IMAGES
of America

PITTSBURGH'S HISTORIC STADIUMS AND ARENAS

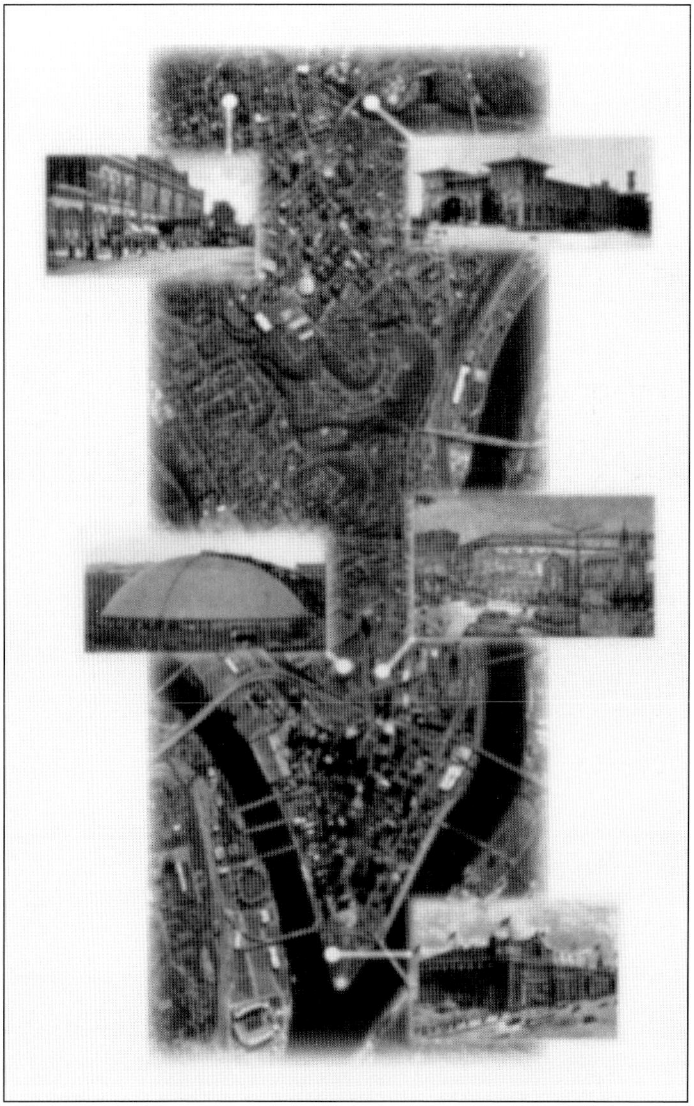

This map shows the location of 130 years of Pittsburgh's hockey venues. This volume will cover the history of these facilities along with Pittsburgh's professional baseball, football, and basketball sites. (Pittsburghhockey.net.)

On the Cover: The 1955 Steelers pose in front of the Forbes Field scoreboard. Primarily remembered as a baseball park, Forbes also hosted pro and college football. Just blocks away, Duquesne Garden was home to professional hockey and basketball. (Pittsburgh Steelers.)

IMAGES
of America

Pittsburgh's Historic Stadiums and Arenas

Mark T. Fatla

ARCADIA
PUBLISHING

ISBN 978-1-4671-6126-8

Published by Arcadia Publishing
Charleston, South Carolina

Printed in the United States of America

Library of Congress Control Number: 2024950955

For all general information, please contact Arcadia Publishing:
Telephone 843-853-2070
Fax 843-853-0044
E-mail sales@arcadiapublishing.com

Visit us on the Internet at www.arcadiapublishing.com

This book is dedicated to my brother Steve, son Zachary, and daughter Allison, who have accompanied me to so many games, from baseball to roller derby, and to my wife, Elaine, for tolerating it and even going along occasionally.

Contents

ACKNOWLEDGMENTS

This book examines the history of the professional baseball, football, hockey, and basketball venues in Pittsburgh. It would not have been possible without many kindnesses in compiling images and accurate historical facts. I have listed sources here (with a key to photograph credits in parentheses and thanks for their courtesy): Gil Pietrzak, Carnegie Library of Pittsburgh (CLP); Dan Hart, Pittsburgh Pirates archives (PP); David Grinnell, University of Pittsburgh Archive (UP); James Kubus, pittsburghhockey.net (PHN); Len Martin, Point 4 (P4); Bob Recker, keeper of the flame for the Ice Capades (Recker); Rob Pfaffmann, Pfaffmann & Associates (PA); Tom White, Duquesne University Archives (DUA); Karl Roser and Jimmy Sacco, Pittsburgh Steelers (PS); Arthur Hundhausen, remembertheaba.com (RABA); Ross Judge, hockeygods.com (HG); Sean Rowland, stadiumandarenavisits.com (SAV); and Craig Britcher and Margaret Hewitt, Heinz History Center (HHC). Other sources include the Library of Congress (LOC), Historic American Buildings Survey (HABS), Carnegie Museum of Art (CMOA), Brookline Library (BL), Photo Antiquities Museum (PAM), Boston Public Library (BPL), Mitchell & Ritchey Architects, Collection at Carnegie-Mellon University Architecture Archives (MRA); Pennsylvania State Archives (PSA), blackfives.com (B5), Squirrel Hill Historical Society (SHHS), Penn State University (PSU), and various Pittsburgh newspapers accessed through newspapers.com. A few contemporary images are provided pursuant to a Creative Commons Attribution (CCA) License and are properly attributed to the creator. Those interested in details or reuse of those images should review the CCA license requirements. Several items are from the author's collection (AC), with most being in the public domain because the first publication occurred prior to January 1, 1929, or due to lack of notice or renewal.

Andy Terrick and Len Martin, Society for American Baseball Research (SABR) members, local historians, and all-around good guys, provided leads, encouragement, and editing to ensure the accuracy of the material to the greatest possible extent. James Kubus provides an invaluable resource with pittsburghhockey.net, and he reviewed the hockey chapters. My son Zachary Fatla provided patient technical help to overcome my considerable technological deficiencies. My wife, Elaine, patiently tolerated the many hours I devoted to this project when I should have been helping her with something.

This book would not have been possible without the knowledge and kindness of the good people listed above and many others. Any errors or omissions are mine alone.

INTRODUCTION

Pittsburgh was often at the forefront of developing sports facilities. Pittsburgh's baseball history is well established. Exposition Park was acclaimed as the finest park of the wooden era. Forbes Field was one of the first concrete and steel parks and has reached near-mythic status in the years since its demolition. Black entrepreneurs in the Hill District were building their own ballparks for Negro League teams. PNC Park is regularly identified as the best of the modern retro-design ballparks. Even the much-maligned Three Rivers Stadium has its place as emblematic of the multiuse concrete bowl stadiums.

The same is true of Pittsburgh's professional football, hockey, and basketball venues. The earliest roots of professional football are firmly planted in Recreation Park, as recognized by the Pro Football Hall of Fame. Long before the concept of multiuse bowls, Pittsburgh's baseball parks were adapted to host the growing popularity of football. In hockey, the first indoor rinks with artificial ice were built in Pittsburgh, resulting in some of the earliest professional teams and leagues. Duquesne Garden was utilitarian but had a long life for both hockey and basketball and also birthed the Ice Capades. The Civic Arena, hosting both hockey and basketball, was a modern engineering marvel, the largest movable dome in the world. Heinz Field and PPG Paints Arena provide the finest amenities to fans and teams and are well regarded in their respective sports.

There are several reasons for this leadership role in sports facilities. Pittsburgh had a can-do attitude about building; after all, this region was building the largest and most complex industrial plants in the world. Its engineers were designing and building an amazing variety of bridges, made with local steel, many still in use today. Local team and venue owners like Barney Dreyfuss of the Pirates, Art Rooney of the Steelers, Gus Greenlee of the Pittsburgh Crawfords, and John H. Harris of Duquesne Garden saw the value in innovative ideas and reinvesting in their facilities. Finally, local colleges like Pitt, Duquesne, and Carnegie-Mellon enjoyed national prominence at different times and in different sports, ensuring a steady stream of athletic and coaching talent and an educated fan base.

The focus here is not on the great players, championship teams, and spectacular plays. There are many other books for that. Instead, the focus is on the venues themselves, how they came to be, and how they evolved over time. I have departed from that to a degree to explain the early days of these sports, when teams, leagues, amateurs, semipros, and professionals make a dizzying kaleidoscope that can be confusing to the casual fan. To provide context for the venues and their use, I have included some images of teams and players and some basic history of those early days, but the focus remains on the venues.

Having to draw a line somewhere, I have limited this book to Pittsburgh venues that were home to pro or semipro teams. Thus, collegiate venues like Pitt Stadium are included primarily to the extent that they hosted a pro team, and amateur venues like Motor Square Garden are necessarily omitted.

This book is limited to baseball, football, hockey, and basketball venues. With Pittsburgh's rich boxing history, a separate volume on the area's indoor and outdoor boxing venues may someday be warranted. Other sports presented at these venues include tennis, soccer, wrestling, cycling, track, roller derby, lacrosse, and indoor football. That also does not account for nonsport uses, like theater, concerts, trade shows, and political rallies. Some of the venues covered in this book were intended to be multiuse, like the Civic Arena and Duquesne Garden. Others were adapted as opportunities arose. A few images of other sports are included in this volume, primarily because they show some aspect of the venue.

One last proviso: the early days of semipro teams and the venues they used are murky at best. This book is not intended to be a definitive list, and the roster of early professional venues may grow with increased research. I hope that this book may stimulate others to explore those early years. Those interested in reading further should visit pittsburghhockey.net, probasketballencyclopedia.com, remembertheaba.com, and hockeygods.com, among others. For a more in-depth view of Pittsburgh's major-league baseball parks, please see my first book, *Pittsburgh's Historic Ballparks* (Arcadia Publishing, 2023).

The search for photographs to illustrate this history included team archives, museums, libraries, newspapers, and private collections. The toughest decisions often involve which images to leave out. I have selected those images that I believe best illustrate the development and evolution of these venues.

As with *Pittsburgh's Historic Ballparks*, I welcome corrections, clarifications, and disagreements. These books are intended to increase the knowledge of these venues and do not purport to be the final word in scholarship and understanding. As additional photographs and historical sources are uncovered, the story of these venues will grow in accuracy and context. The story continues.

One

Baseball Parks

Pittsburgh's rich history of major-league ballparks dates back to the 1870s. The earliest wooden grandstand was erected at Union Park in Allegheny, now Pittsburgh's North Side. In 1884, a new double-deck grandstand was built on the same grounds, and in 1885, it was renamed Recreation Park. The Pittsburgh Alleghenys made this their home park in 1884 and joined the National League in 1887.

Exposition Park was built in 1890 near the Allegheny River to serve a new team in the Players League. When the league folded after one season, the Alleghenys moved in and became known as the Pirates. Exposition Park was one of the best of the wooden-era ballparks, and despite annual spring flooding, it was home to the Pirates until 1909.

The construction of Forbes Field and Philadelphia's Shibe Park kicked off a building boom of modern concrete and steel ballparks that gave us such icons as Wrigley Field, Fenway Park, and Yankee Stadium. Through expansions, alterations, renovations, and finally neglect, Forbes would be home to the Pirates for 61 seasons. Each year, hundreds of fans gather on October 13 in front of the remnants of the outfield wall to listen to a rebroadcast of Game 7 of the 1960 World Series.

In its shameful segregated history, baseball relegated African American ballplayers to the Negro Leagues. In Pittsburgh, black entrepreneurs built their own ballparks and assembled some of the greatest teams in baseball history, black or white.

Opened in 1970, Three Rivers Stadium was emblematic of the "concrete bowl" era of multiuse stadiums. Without any of the charm and quirks of Forbes Field, Three Rivers was unloved, but it was home to the Pirates and Steelers when they made Pittsburgh the "City of Champions."

PNC Park did not begin the "retro-ballpark" movement but may represent its pinnacle. With its small size, close-to-the-action seats, and a spectacular view of Downtown, it is regularly touted as the finest ballpark of the new millennium. This chapter provides a brief overview of Pittsburgh's major-league ballparks.

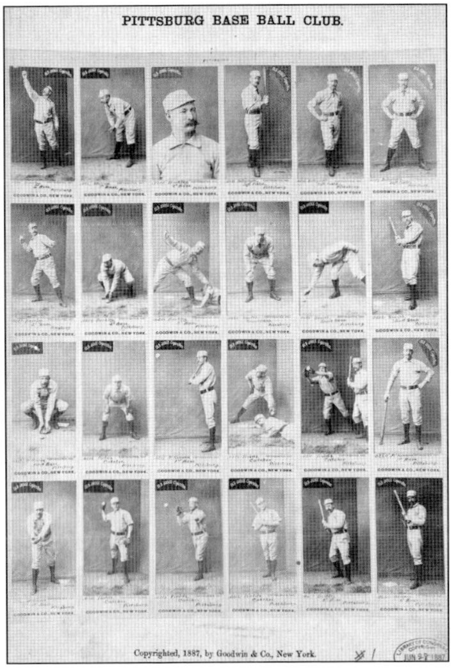

The Pittsburgh Alleghenys formed in 1882 to compete in the American Association. They started play on the old Exposition grounds along the river, but by 1884, flooding pushed them to Union Park, where a new grandstand was built and named Recreation Park. Although the franchise began in 1882, current Pirates management sometimes dates their origin to their 1887 entry into the National League (NL). That first NL team is depicted in Old Judge tobacco cards. (LOC.)

This is the only known photograph of the Recreation Park grandstand. Though taken in 1894, after the Alleghenys moved to Exposition Park, this is the ballpark that was home to the Alleghenys from 1884 to 1890. The photograph was discovered in 2015 in the cornerstone of a building during demolition. Though distant and indistinct, the image reveals a curved double-deck grandstand. A simple wooden fence of vertical planks encloses the grounds. (HHC.)

In 1884, the Toledo Blues (also known as "Bluestockings") played the Pittsburgh Alleghenys at Recreation Park. The Blues' regular catcher was Moses Fleetwood "Fleet" Walker (third row, center). Walker was the first African American to play a major-league game in Pittsburgh. By 1885, the color line descended over baseball, and no black man would play in the white major leagues until Jackie Robinson in 1947. (AC.)

TOLEDO NORTHWESTERN LEAGUE CHAMPION CLUB—1883

BACK ROW—Joseph A. Miller, Dr. Daniel A. Jones, Moses Fleetwood Walker, George M. "Chappy" Lane, John C. Tilley.
MIDDLE ROW—Samuel R. Moffet, Samuel W. Barkley—Captain, Charles H. Morton—Manager, Curtis B. Welch, Henry M. "Hank" O'Day.
FRONT ROW—Thomas J. Poorman and Horace Lockwood.

The Alleghenys shared Recreation Park in 1887 with the Pittsburgh Keystones, the first Negro League team in Pittsburgh. Their second baseman was 19-year-old King Solomon "Sol" White. Sadly, the league folded in two weeks. The Keystones continued as an independent team, but White (back row, second from left) moved on to the integrated Wheeling team. His career as a player, a manager, and the first historian of black baseball led him to baseball's hall of fame. (Gitterman Gallery.)

The 1889 Alleghenys pose in front of the grandstand at Recreation Park. The front row of seats is raised about five feet above the playing field. As was common at that time, seating consisted of individual bent-back chairs rather than fixed seating. The 1889 team finished fifth in the eight-team league. Hall of fame pitcher Pud Galvin is seated at the far left with his arms crossed. (PP.)

The Alleghenys moved to Exposition Park in 1891 after the failure of the Players League, but success on the field was elusive, as seen in this 1891 newspaper cartoon. The artist's sketch of the grandstand, though not to scale, accurately includes the rooftop boxes, the "Y" bracing on the columns, and the pyramid roof on the stair tower. (*Press.*)

The 1897 team poses in front of an unidentified structure on the grounds of Exposition Park. This may be the clubhouse where the players dressed. The 1897 team continued the run of futility, finishing 8th in the 12-team league, 32.5 games out of first. (PP.)

Things began to look up in 1900 when Barney Dreyfuss bought an ownership stake in the Pirates and brought along the best players from his failing Louisville team, including a young Honus Wagner (back row, second from right). The 1900 team finished second, and the 1901 club, posed here in a studio, won the first of three straight NL pennants. Excited crowds filled Exposition Park. (PP.)

From deep in the outfield in 1905, the full Exposition Park grandstand is visible with its rooftop boxes and the pyramid roofs of the stair towers. For overflow crowds, ropes were strung in the outfield for fans to stand behind. The burgeoning popularity of baseball meant there were thousands of fans willing to pay for a standing-room ticket, and management was not going to turn them away. (PP.)

The first modern World Series was played in 1903 at Exposition Park and the Huntington Grounds in Boston (the forerunner to Fenway Park). A rabid group of Boston fans, known as the Royal Rooters, traveled to Pittsburgh for the games and made a loud nuisance of themselves by endlessly singing their theme song, "Tessie." The gang is posed with their team in their seats on the third-base side of the Exposition Park grandstand. (BPL.)

This view from the right-field bleachers provides a great look at the third-base side of the grandstand and the smoky city skyline beyond. More than 100 years before PNC Park, Exposition Park had a view of Downtown, albeit largely obscured by the haze of the city's polluted atmosphere. (PP.)

One thing doomed Exposition Park—the annual flooding from the Allegheny River. Before flood controls on the rivers, Downtown and the low-lying areas of the city of Allegheny were inundated nearly every spring. Pirates owner Barney Dreyfuss eventually found dry land in Oakland to build Forbes Field. (BL.)

On Louisa Street during the inaugural week of Forbes Field, newsboys sell papers and souvenir photographs. Construction is not yet complete—tarpaulins cover the upper-level openings where windows have not yet been installed. It did not discourage fans. More than 30,000 attended the inaugural game on June 30, 1909. (LOC.)

The new Forbes Field grandstand is seen from deep center field during its inaugural game on June 30, 1909. The overflow crowd was accommodated behind ropes in the outfield. The park included such innovations as ramps, telephones, an elevator, a room for the umpires, and a clubhouse for the visiting team. It was built in just four months. During the 1909 World Series, Dreyfuss became the first to provide a free spread to feed the baseball writers. (AC.)

FORBES FIELD, PITTSBURGH, PA. OPENING DAY JUNE 30TH, 1909, ATTENDANCE 30338

The main entrance at the corner of Louisa and Boquet (sometimes spelled "Bouquet") Streets is pictured with construction completed. Decorative details around windows and in the arches, columns, and awning over the main entrance, along with Dreyfuss's ban on billboard advertising, earned the ballpark high praise for beauty and refinement. The arches on the ground floor were a memorable defining element of the park and were later reflected in PNC Park. (PP.)

Though Forbes Field had greater seating capacity than Exposition Park, big games still created overflow crowds that were accommodated with standing room on the field. This view of the inaugural 1909 game shows crowds packed in front of, and seated on, the outfield wall. The scoreboard and flagpole are at right. In the distance are the Carnegie Library and Museum. (R.W. Johnston.)

Before the 1925 season, Dreyfuss completed the largest expansion in the park's history, extending the first-base grandstand and adding the towering right-field pavilion, seen at top right. Despite the increased capacity, temporary bleachers were built in front of and over the outfield walls for the 1925 World Series, and the scoreboard was moved to the left-field corner. The Pirates defeated the Washington Senators in seven games. (PP.)

For the 1927 World Series, temporary bleachers were erected above and behind the outfield walls but no longer on the field, as in 1925. The scoreboard is seen in the left-field corner. Also evident in this view from atop the grandstand is the large amount of foul ground around the infield. The "Murderers' Row" Yankees with Babe Ruth and Lou Gehrig swept the Pirates in four games. (PP.)

While the Pirates played in the whites-only major leagues, black entrepreneurs organized the Negro Leagues. In 1920, Alexander McDonald Williams built a wooden grandstand he named Central Amusement Park. It was the first ballpark in the country owned, designed, and built by African Americans, and this is the only known photograph. Williams entered his Pittsburgh Keystones in the Negro National League in 1922, but it was a financial disaster. The ballpark was demolished in 1925. (UP.)

In the 1920s, Gus Greenlee, numbers kingpin and owner of the famed Crawford Grill, provided financial support for the Crawfords, a local semipro team. Greenlee began recruiting the best black ballplayers in the country to join his team. He and his white partners built Greenlee Field, seen here behind the team bus. The Crawfords became a national powerhouse with stars like Satchel Paige and Josh Gibson. The ballpark only lasted from 1932 to 1938. (PP.)

This dramatic view is from the top deck of Forbes Field's right-field pavilion. Built in 1925, it was the largest expansion in the park's history. Other significant changes were the Crow's Nest on the grandstand roof behind home, added in 1938, and permanent light towers installed in 1940. Field-level seating was increased several times, extending forward into foul ground. (PP.)

Players enjoy a relaxed moment in the Forbes Field locker room. Roberto Clemente is seated at left. Each stall had a stationary swivel chair and little else. Luggage is stacked on top. A suitcase marked "21" is atop Clemente's locker at left next to the door. From the uniform style and the player names on the lockers, this is 1955 or 1956. (PP.)

This is how Forbes Field is typically remembered, in its final decade with the scoreboard topped by the Longines clock, the light towers, and the lush green of Schenley Park beyond the ivy-covered walls. Hemmed in by a growing University of Pittsburgh hungry for land, Forbes Field was doomed. The Pirates moved to Three Rivers Stadium in 1970, and Forbes was demolished in 1971. (PSA.)

In the late stages of demolition in 1971, about all that remains are the left-field line bleachers and the scoreboard, dominated by Pitt's Cathedral of Learning. Today, home plate and a portion of the outfield wall remain. One can visit the wall in the early afternoon of October 13 each year to relive Game 7 of the 1960 World Series with a few hundred other crazy baseball fans. (UP.)

This unique aerial view shows the outline of a Fort Pitt bastion (constructed in 1760) in Point State Park while Three Rivers Stadium is under construction across the river more than 200 years later. The double-arch Manchester Bridge is still standing at top left. It would be removed in the fall of 1970. The sculptures from its north portal now stand near Stage AE. (PP.)

Planning for a new stadium had been underway since the early 1950s, and Pitt purchased Forbes Field in 1958 with the understanding that the Pirates could remain until a new ballpark was ready. The new stadium opened on July 16, 1970, and the opening game ticket had an image of the new park and Downtown. The price of this upper-deck ticket was $3.15. (AC.)

A major goal of city leaders was to rejuvenate the North Side—or at least that portion of the old city of Allegheny along the river. The former site of Exposition Park had become a massive scrap yard, and the riverfront was a post-industrial disaster. This 1975 Allegheny Chamber of Commerce booklet promoted its redevelopment vision. (AC.)

A full house packs the stadium for a night game. Downtown office towers peek up over the rim of the stadium. During the design phase, an open-ended stadium with a view of Downtown was sacrificed for more seats and lower construction costs. The result was a large concrete bowl typical of that era. (PP.)

Three Rivers Stadium was certainly photogenic, especially at night when paired with the fountain at the Point. While the concrete bowl with the plastic grass was unloved by many, it was a major step in reorienting the city to its rivers and shedding the old "Smoky City" image. The site of home plate has been marked in a parking lot by local SABR members. (PP.)

PNC Park opened in 2000 and is universally acknowledged as a great ballpark in the retro-design style. It has the view that Three Rivers never had while providing all the modern amenities and maintaining an intimate size. Statues of Wagner, Clemente, Mazeroski, and Stargell stand at various entry gates. (LOC-Highsmith.)

Two

Football Stadiums

In the fall of 1892, two amateur clubs, the Allegheny Athletic Association (AAA) and the Pittsburgh Athletic Club (PAC), played to a scoreless tie. A rematch was set for November 12, 1892, at Recreation Park, and both teams sought an edge. Early college football star William "Pudge" Heffelfinger entertained offers from both clubs. Allegheny won the bidding, and Pudge proved his worth, causing a fumble and scoring the game's only touchdown. Allegheny paid Pudge his fee of $500 and recorded the payment in the club ledger. The Pro Football Hall of Fame recognizes this as the earliest documented instance of someone being paid to play football.

Western Pennsylvania was a national hot spot for pro football in the 1890s. There were top teams in Greensburg, Latrobe, Pitcairn, and Jeanette, as well as Pittsburgh and Allegheny, and fierce rivalries developed. Pittsburgh's firsts include the first team to openly pay its players, the first fully professional team to complete a full season, the first individual to own a football team, and the first professional league.

College football ultimately proved to be more popular than the pros. Colleges provided more organizational and financial stability than the individual athletic clubs, and alumni provided a natural fan base. Pro and semipro teams played as independents, scheduling opponents that could draw a crowd. There were no viable professional leagues until the founding of the National Football League in 1920.

Baseball and football teams often shared the same grounds. With the popularity of baseball, early stadiums were built primarily to serve baseball teams. Football clubs had to make do and shoehorn their fields into the ballparks. For example, in an era when a standard football field measured 110 yards, Recreation Park could only accommodate a 100-yard field. Football's growing popularity and its need to provide better seating for fans ultimately drove the move to multiuse stadiums like Three Rivers and football-only venues like Pitt Stadium and Heinz Field.

This chapter focuses on the football usage of Pittsburgh venues. For a full history of these venues built for baseball, see *Pittsburgh's Historic Ballparks* (Arcadia Publishing, 2023).

Recreation Park in the city of Allegheny (today part of Pittsburgh's North Side) was primarily known as a baseball field, but it also hosted many early pro and amateur football games. Here, the 1899 team of the Western University of Pennsylvania (WUP, later renamed the University of Pittsburgh) poses on the field with the outfield fence in the background. (UP.)

The original curved-front grandstand that stood when the Alleghenys played baseball gave way at some point to the grandstand seen here. This view of an October 1902 WUP game at Recreation Park shows a straight, two-tiered wooden grandstand with "X" bracing between support columns. The land and open-air bleachers slope slightly upward to the right. (*Dispatch.*)

In 1902, the first professional football league was formed. The National Football League (no relation to today's NFL) had two teams in Philadelphia and one in Pittsburgh. In Pittsburgh, it occupied Recreation Park to prevent the upstart American League from obtaining grounds for a competing baseball club. The Pittsburgh Stars were comprised of the best players from local pro teams, plus New York Giants pitching star Christy Mathewson, who played halfback. (Keystone College.)

Though the Stars played home games at Recreation Park, they practiced in Greensburg, Pennsylvania, earning the resentment of fans and sportswriters who could not see the new club until game days. It did not bother the players. They won the title in the league's only season with a win at Recreation Park, seen here in game action on November 30, 1902. It is not clear when the park was demolished, but by 1910, the land was occupied by industrial uses. (*Press.*)

THE DUQUESNE COUNTRY AND ATHLETIC CLUB FOOTBALL TEAM.

Built in 1890, Exposition Park soon became home to the Pirates baseball team and many of the early football clubs, like Duquesne Country and Athletic Club. They played from 1895 to 1900, typically using Exposition Park for home games. They may have been the best pro team in the country. Here, the 1899 team poses in front of the right-field bleachers and first-base grandstand. (*Bulletin*.)

D. C. & A. C. FOOTBALL TEAM OF 1900.—PHOTOGRAPH BY R. W. JOHNSTON & CO.

Those Duquesne boys liked to pose for team photographs. Here is the 1900 squad at Exposition Park. Behind them are the empty left-field bleachers and billboards on the outfield fence. Exposition Park was conveniently located near rail lines and streetcar lines, just across the river from the city of Pittsburgh, thereby ensuring good crowds for early professional teams. (AC.)

The Duquesne team lines up for the kick-off at Exposition Park in November 1900 with quite a crowd in the bleachers. William Chase Temple, a local steel magnate and former owner of the Pirates baseball team, provided financial backing for the club and thus became the first individual owner of a pro football team. Note the advertising on the outfield fence. (*Press.*)

The WUP team also moved its home games to Exposition Park. The field was a very popular site for both pro and amateur football teams while also hosting Wild West Shows, circuses, and an annual soccer tournament. Here, the 1905 WUP team poses in front of the grandstand. (UP.)

African Americans also organized amateur and semipro football teams like the Collins Tigers, seen here on wooden bleachers at an unidentified field in 1912–1913. Some clubs played at Exposition Park, which was also the site of an annual Thanksgiving Day game between African American teams. (HHC.)

SNAP SHOTS AT HOMESTEAD STARS PREPARING FOR YESTERDAY'S GAME.

TOMMY RYAN SIGNS TO MEET EDDIE KENNEDY.

Steelworks Park in Homestead was home to both the Homestead Library and Athletic Club (HLAC) and the Murdock Grays, later known as the Homestead Grays and more famous for their baseball team. The HLAC posted two consecutive undefeated seasons from 1900 to 1902, making them the top pro football team in the country. HLAC players would dress at the nearby Homestead Library and play at the field located across the rail lines from the massive steel plant. (*Press*.)

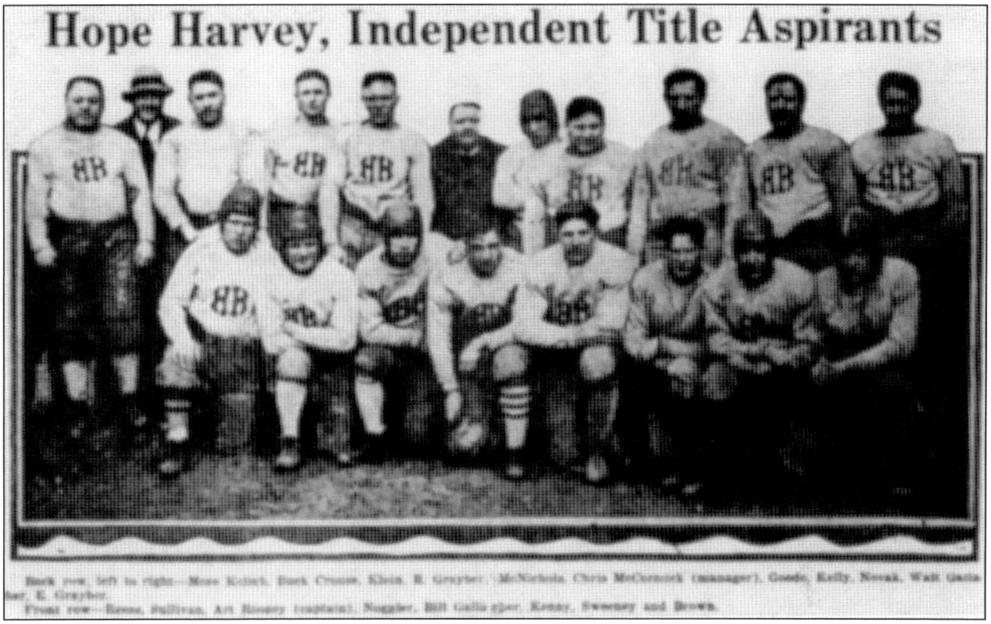

In the 1920s, a young North Side athlete organized an independent semipro football team named Hope-Harvey after its sponsors. The team played at Exposition Park and drew good crowds, with reportedly as many as 12,000 spectators. The founder served as player-coach and recruited athletes for the team, including his brothers. Arthur J. "Art" Rooney (first row, third from left) would go on to found the Pittsburgh Steelers. (*Post*.)

Fed up with repeated flooding and limited capacity at Exposition Park, Pirates owner Barney Dreyfuss built a new concrete and steel park in Oakland named Forbes Field. This construction photograph shows the steel frame taking shape. The ballpark was built in just four months in early 1909 and served as the home of the Pirates for 61 years (P4.)

Forbes Field also had a long history with football. Local colleges played here, most notably the newly relocated WUP, renamed the University of Pittsburgh. This panorama of a game between Pitt and Washington & Jefferson College on November 6, 1915, shows the grandstand, the

permanent left-field line bleachers, and temporary football bleachers down the right-field line and in left field. Because Dreyfuss disliked home runs, he built a park with a large outfield that also made a football field possible on the grounds. (LOC.)

The University of Pittsburgh moved from the city of Allegheny to Oakland in 1909, and the football team moved from Exposition Park to Forbes Field. While the team had considerable success at Exposition Park, Pitt became a national power in its first decade at Forbes Field. The 1910 team, posed here on the temporary bleachers set up in left field for football games, was unbeaten and unscored upon. (UP.)

The elements were still an issue. Here, students clear Forbes Field of snow before a 1914 Pitt game. The left-field line bleachers are seen at left. While Pitt prospered at Forbes, university leaders saw other schools developing large football-only stadiums on campus, so they began planning Pitt Stadium, which would open in 1925. In the 1930s, Forbes would be home to the Duquesne Dukes football team as it rose to national prominence. (AC.)

The NFL was organized in 1920 but had no Pennsylvania teams because state "blue laws" prohibited sporting events on Sundays. In 1933, with the repeal of the blue laws imminent, Art Rooney applied for an NFL franchise. For an entry fee of $2,500, Rooney was approved and set about organizing a team known as the Pirates. This is the inaugural 1933 team with a young Art Rooney in a suit (second row, far left). (PS.)

During the 1930s, Rooney's football Pirates practiced at Greenlee Field, the Negro League ballpark in Pittsburgh's Hill District, home to the Pittsburgh Crawfords and Homestead Grays. It also accommodated football, as shown in this newspaper photograph. The grandstand is at the bottom, the distant hillside top to the right has bleachers and a fence, and the scoreboard is on the left-field wall. The park was sold and demolished in 1938 to make way for public housing. (*Courier.*)

In 1936, the American Football League (AFL) was organized to compete with the NFL. The Pittsburgh Americans had the awkward nickname "Amerks" and played home games at Forbes Field in 1936 and 1937, sharing it with Rooney's NFL Pirates. The Amerks were a mediocre team and averaged only 2,500 fans per game. After losing their first three league games in 1937, the team folded. At the end of that season, so did the AFL. (*Sun-Telegraph.*)

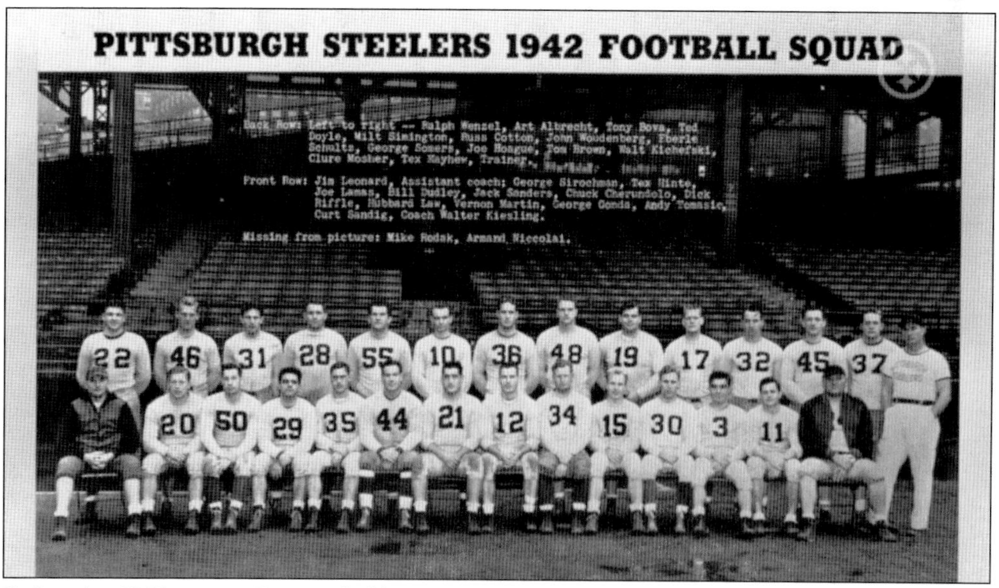

Before the 1940 season, Rooney held a contest to rename his team. Fourteen people suggested "Steelers." The 1942 Steelers pose in front of the grandstand at Forbes Field. The steel structure and its innovative ramps are visible. In the 10th year of the franchise, the team had its first winning season, going 7-4-0 to finish second in the NFL East. However, times were about to get tough. (PS.)

During World War II, NFL teams faced a serious manpower shortage. The Steelers and Philadelphia Eagles combined rosters for the 1943 season to create the Steagles, seen in this montage. Most players had various physical conditions that made them ineligible for military service. For example, Tony Bova led the team in receiving but was blind in one eye. All players were required to work full-time war jobs, but despite this, the team finished 5-4-1. (PS.)

The 1943 Steagles are seen in game action at Forbes Field. The scoreboard and Carnegie Library are in the background. In 1944, the Eagles resumed play as a separate team, while the Steelers joined with the Chicago Cardinals to form the "Card-Pitt" team. They went winless in 10 games, earning the nickname "Carpets," and were dubbed "the worst team in NFL history" by Art Rooney. In both years, the conjoined teams split their home games between cities. (PS.)

The Steelers are seen here in action at Forbes Field in the 1950s. The scoreboard with the round Gruen clock is in the background. Forbes Field would be the Steelers' home field from 1933 to 1957. From 1958 to 1963, the team split home games between Forbes and Pitt Stadium. (P4.)

This aerial photograph from the late 1940s or early 1950s shows the position of the gridiron at Forbes Field and illustrates why a baseball park is a bad fit for football. The greatest number of seats are behind the end zones. There are few seats near the 50-yard line. The bleachers down the left-field line are far from the field. (PAM.)

From the uniform styles and the Greenberg Garden fence in front of the left-field wall, this game against the New York Giants is from the early 1950s. The scoreboard has the round Gruen clock and the square Western Union game clock. The Young Men's Hebrew Association (YMHA) Building, which once hosted pro basketball (see chapter five), is seen beyond the left-field foul pole. (P4.)

Game action at Forbes Field in 1954 is dramatically highlighted by the autumn sun shining through the steel frame of the stadium. Paul Cameron makes the interception. Cameron only played one season for the Steelers but made the Pro Bowl. The baseball dugout and a photographer are visible behind the players. Note the flag at far right marking the corner of the end zone. (PS.)

This game action versus the Browns dates to the mid-1950s based on the single-bar face masks on the helmets. Again, the scoreboard features prominently in this view. The ivy on the outfield wall has died back for winter, revealing the brick. Originally made of wood, the outfield walls in left and center were rebuilt in brick in 1946. (P4.)

The 1957 Steelers pose in front of the Forbes Field scoreboard. The name on the round clock was changed to "Forbes Field" after previous sponsor Gruen went out of business. In 1959, it would be replaced by a square Longines clock. The square Western Union clock at right kept the game time. The scoreboard is ready for a college game between Carnegie and Westminster, while the Steelers game against the New York Giants on December 7 is advertised. The 1957 team finished 6-6. (PS.)

An undated game from the 1950s provides an excellent view from behind the visitors' bench to the right-field pavilion. The Steelers bench was on the same side of the field, out of view to the left. The football press box is atop the roof at right center. (P4.)

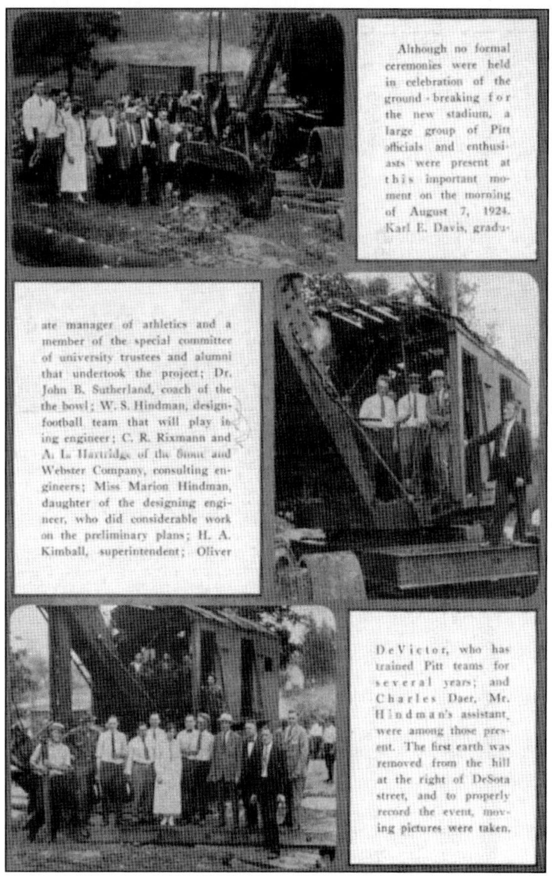

Although no formal ceremonies were held in celebration of the ground-breaking for the new stadium, a large group of Pitt officials and enthusiasts were present at this important moment on the morning of August 7, 1924. Karl E. Davis, graduate manager of athletics and a member of the special committee of university trustees and alumni that undertook the project; Dr. John B. Sutherland, coach of the the bowl; W. S. Hindman, design-football team that will play in ing engineer; C. R. Rixmann and A. L. Hartridge of the Stone and Webster Company, consulting engineers; Miss Marion Hindman, daughter of the designing engineer, who did considerable work on the preliminary plans; H. A. Kimball, superintendent; Oliver DeVictor, who has trained Pitt teams for several years; and Charles Daer, Mr. Hindman's assistant, were among those present. The first earth was removed from the hill at the right of DeSota street, and to properly record the event, moving pictures were taken.

As Pitt football grew in success and national reputation from 1910 to the early 1920s, Forbes Field's limitations became painfully obvious. University leadership saw a need for a dedicated on-campus facility designed for football. As reported in the *Owl*, the Pitt yearbook, there was no formal ground-breaking ceremony for Pitt Stadium, but that did not stop football fans from coming out to mark the occasion. (UP.)

The university acquired nine hillside acres that became known as "Cardiac Hill." Here, the steel frame of the seating bowl is taking shape and the exterior skin is being applied. Total construction time was a little more than a year with the first game on September 26, 1925, a 26-0 Pitt victory over Washington and Lee. The total cost of acquisition and construction was $1.2 million. (UP.)

The 1939 Pitt team poses in front of the empty stands. At top are the scoreboard and clock. The 1939 team was the first without hall of fame coach Jock Sutherland and finished with a 5-4 record, including its last game against crosstown rival Duquesne, a 21-13 loss. (UP.)

As built, Pitt Stadium could seat 69,400 with temporary bleachers surrounding the field, as seen here in 1945. The stadium was designed with an option to add a second deck for an additional 30,000 seats, which would have made it the first mega-stadium, but while Pitt drew well, ticket demand never justified expansion, and the university de-emphasized football by 1940. (CLP.)

By 1949, the elimination of temporary bleachers and widening of existing seats reduced capacity to 56,500, and that remained constant until the stadium closed in 1999. This 1951 aerial of Oakland puts Pitt Stadium and other sports venues in context. The Cathedral of Learning is at the center with the YMHA behind it. Forbes Field is at the right edge. St. Paul's Cathedral, with its twin spires, is at left, blocking the view of Duquesne Garden. (UP.)

In 1958, Pitt purchased Forbes Field to provide space for expansion but allowed the Pirates to remain until a new stadium was built. No one expected that to take 12 years, but Three Rivers Stadium did not open until the summer of 1970. Beginning in 1958, the Steelers chose to move select home games to Pitt Stadium with its larger capacity and better sight lines for football. (PS.)

The Steelers enter Pitt Stadium from the tunnel in the corner of the end zone. Stencils of panthers and Greek fraternity/sorority letters on the walls are a reminder that the pro team had no home of its own. The stands consist of simple bench seating. A small set of temporary bleachers is against the wall. (PS.)

Players stand on the sidelines at Pitt Stadium. The bench and water coolers are at right, and the entrance tunnel is beyond that. It looks like a good-size crowd on this day. From 1958 to 1963, the Steelers split their home games between Forbes Field and Pitt Stadium. Fans could buy ticket packages for either venue or both. In 1964, the team moved all home games to Pitt Stadium until Three Rivers Stadium opened in 1970. (PS.)

In this image, the Steelers lead the Bears 24-13 at Pitt Stadium in the season opener on September 17, 1967, in front of 53,565. The Steelers would win 41-13 despite a 103-yard kick return by Gale Sayers. The "Welcome to Pitt Stadium" sign is visible on the wall at the bottom of the seating bowl, and the scoreboard is seen at top. (PS.)

Game action from September 15, 1968, shows a crowd of 45,698 for the season opener against the New York Giants. The Giants No. 10 is Fran Tarkenton. Pitt Stadium was not kind to the Steelers. After abandoning Forbes Field and moving all home games to Pitt Stadium in 1964, the team suffered six straight losing seasons, culminating in a 1-13 record in 1969, its last at Pitt Stadium but first under new coach Chuck Noll. (PS.)

The Steelerettes were the first cheerleading squad in the NFL and performed at Steeler games from 1961 to 1969. Here, they are at Pitt Stadium. They were disbanded in 1969, and to this day, the Steelers remain one of the few NFL teams without cheerleaders. (BL.)

While professional football left in 1970, Pitt Stadium continued to host Pitt football until November 13, 1999, when Pitt defeated Notre Dame 37-27. Demolition began just one month later. The stadium site is now occupied by the Petersen Events Center and student housing. (UP.)

After World War II, civic leadership began to pursue new sports venues as a means to change Pittsburgh's image and remain competitive with other urban centers. One of the more extravagant concepts floated in the 1950s was this stadium suspended over the Monongahela River. It appeared on a promotional postcard. It was fun to dream about, but it does not appear that this idea was ever taken seriously. (AC.)

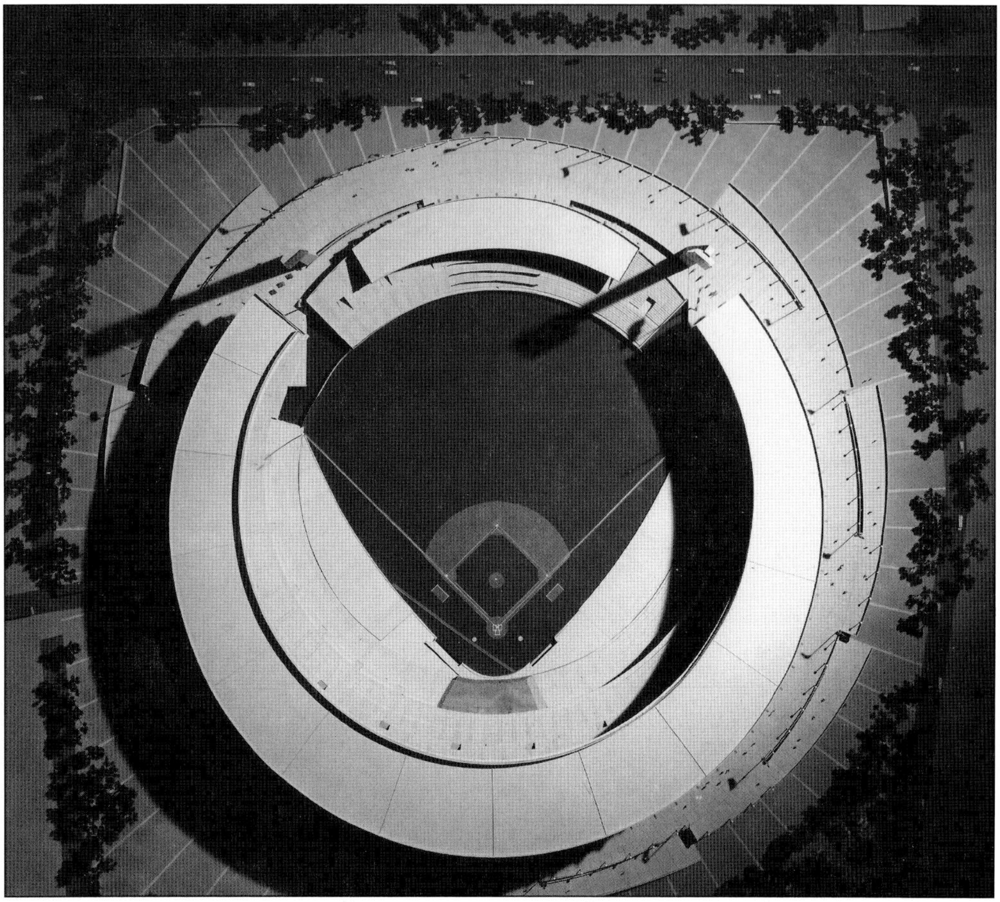

More realistic but still innovative ideas were pursued. This 1964 planning model shows an open-ended stadium with a movable seating section in the open end that could slide forward to a position along the football sideline. Here is the baseball configuration with the seating pushed back in center field. This concept was abandoned due to cost considerations and because the Steelers wanted more seats, particularly at midfield. (PP.)

A 1967 model shows the fully enclosed circular bowl that emerged from the design process and became Three Rivers Stadium. Like other concrete stadiums of the 1960s and 1970s, it served both baseball and football, promised fewer weather postponements with artificial turf, and provided the teams with profitable luxury boxes and expanded concessions. (PP.)

Three Rivers is seen here in 1995 in its football configuration with a full house of 59,000 Steeler fans. The Steelers played their final game here on December 16, 2000, beating Washington 24-3. The stadium had lasted only 30 years and was imploded on February 11, 2001. The public debt was not retired until 2010. (escapedtowisconsin.)

"The Chief," Art Rooney, poses in his office at Three Rivers with his son Dan. Behind Art is a panorama of Exposition Park, where he played football as a youngster, just a block from his home above his father's saloon. Also on the wall are photographs of his wife, Kathleen, former mayor and governor David Lawrence, and other mementos. The Chief passed in 1988. Dan succeeded him as Steeler president and passed in 2017. (PS.)

The ground-breaking for Heinz Field occurred on June 18, 1999. It took two years and $281 million to build it. Here, a doomed Three Rivers remains while its replacement is under construction. Also in this view, the Monongahela (top left) and the Allegheny (lower left) join to form the Ohio (right). Heinz Field opened in 2001, and its first football game was a Steeler preseason victory over the Detroit Lions on August 25, 2001. (PS.)

Three Rivers Stadium was imploded on the morning of February 11, 2001. Heinz Field stands at far left, just 80 feet from the old stadium and undamaged by the implosion. The Steelers erected a monument at the site of Franco Harris's Immaculate Reception, and the Forbes Field chapter of the Society for American Baseball Research marked the location of the pitcher's mound, second base, and home plate with commemorative plaques. (PS.)

Like Three Rivers, Heinz Field enjoys a dramatic riverside location, and like Pitt Stadium, it is a football-only facility shared by the Steelers and the University of Pittsburgh. Here it is in 2018. The Point Fountain marks the confluence. The Mister Rogers Memorial, constructed from a pier of the old Manchester Bridge, stands along the river at right center. (Alex Liivet.)

The Steelers and the Sports and Exhibition Authority (SEA) have continued to reinvest in the stadium, with renovations in 2007 and expanded seating and amenities under the scoreboard at the south end zone in 2015. However, disappointing attendance for Pitt games had the university thinking once again about an on-campus facility. This view is from 2019. In 2022, the name changed to Acrisure Stadium. (Tony Webster.)

This 2007 photograph provides a rare look inside the team locker room at Heinz Field. The helmet hanging in Casey Hampton's locker is part of a throwback uniform mimicking the yellow helmets of the 1950s. (Steel City Hobbies.)

Located outside the southwest corner of the stadium is a small quiet plaza with a statue of the Chief, Art Rooney, looking relaxed and ready to swap stories. A lifelong North Sider, his home still stands a short walk away in the Allegheny West neighborhood. Behind the statue is a relic of Three Rivers Stadium, the Gate D pylon. (TheZachMorrisExperience.)

Three

Early Hockey Arenas

Evolving in Canada and New England, ice hockey was a seasonal outdoor sport played on frozen ponds and rivers. In 1862, the Victoria Skating Rink was built in Montreal as the first indoor rink in the world but with a natural ice surface. That meant that skating remained a seasonal event, and the structure hosted other events and exhibitions during warmer months. On March 3, 1875, the first indoor hockey game was played on its rink.

In Pittsburgh, skating had become a popular recreation, and Union Park in the city of Allegheny, now Pittsburgh's North Side, was flooded in the winter to create an ice surface. The growing sport of baseball soon overtook skating in popularity, and Union Park was converted to a baseball diamond, hosting Pittsburgh's first professional baseball team. It was later rechristened Recreation Park.

The seasonal nature of ice and the outdoor discomforts for spectators limited the spread of hockey. Since 1893, Pittsburgh had been toying with the idea of building a multipurpose venue to host theater, concerts, and other social events, but the concept languished until entertainment industry entrepreneur James Conant convinced his employer Harry Davis and local political boss Christopher Lyman Magee that an indoor rink with ice created by mechanical means was possible. With Magee's backing, investors flocked to the concept, and the Schenley Park Casino opened in Pittsburgh in 1895 as the first indoor rink in North America with artificial ice.

This innovation spurred the start of professional hockey as Canadian players sought opportunities to play a longer season in front of comfortable paying fans. At the same time that professional football was taking root across the river in Allegheny, Pittsburgh was giving birth to professional hockey.

With $400,000 in financing, the Schenley Park Casino was an outstanding architectural achievement, including 18-foot-tall Palladian windows, 1,500 incandescent lights, two tiers of seating, luxury boxes, a theater, a café, a merry-go-round, and a rooftop garden. To create ice, a series of chiller pipes were laid down and covered with concrete to create a watertight bowl. Ammonia gas was pumped through the pipes, freezing the concrete and an inch of water on top. (CLP.)

An interior view of the ice rink reveals the balcony encircling the rink and the grand arched windows. The casino was located at the entrance to Schenley Park, next to a temporary wooden bridge that spanned Junction Hollow. Today, the Frick Fine Arts Building stands on this site, next to the Mary Schenley Fountain. The Schenley Bridge, opened in 1898 to replace the wooden bridge, now connects to Phipps Conservatory across the ravine. (HG.)

Visitors entered the building at the balcony level, 20 feet above the ice surface, which was below ground. Private boxes for politicians and wealthy businessmen stood at either end of the balcony. At ice level, three rows of wooden benches with velvet cushions encircled the rink. Capacity was more than 12,000. The building opened on May 29, 1895. (CLP.)

NEGROES ADMITTED TO THE CASINO NOW.

IT IS EVEN ASSERTED THAT THEY WERE NEVER DISCRIMINATED AGAINST.

CERTAIN PEOPLE EXCLUDED.

The Manager Claims the Right to Be Choice About His Visitors.

ALL BAD CHARACTERS BARRED.

The casino immediately attracted a firestorm of controversy when it refused admission to African Americans. Protest meetings were held, ministers gave fiery sermons, and political pressure was exerted on Pittsburgh's ruling Republican Party. As reported in this August 21, 1895, headline, the casino managers denied discriminating and publicly assured Pittsburgh's minority community that it was welcome, though the listed exceptions made that ring hollow. (*Post*.)

This view of an 1895 team on the ice at the casino is the earliest known photograph of hockey in Pittsburgh. The first game was played at the casino on December 30, 1895, with local players pitted against visitors from Queens University of Canada in a 90-minute exhibition. The ice sheet was 300 feet long, compared to the 200 feet of modern NHL rinks. (PHN.)

A close-up view of the first hockey team reveals some of the details of the casino's ornate columns, electric lighting, and the staircase to the balcony. James Conant, the guiding hand behind the casino's development, stands at rear in his bowler hat. Note the team is posed with a ball instead of a puck, likely for an early variation of ice hockey called "bandy." (HG.)

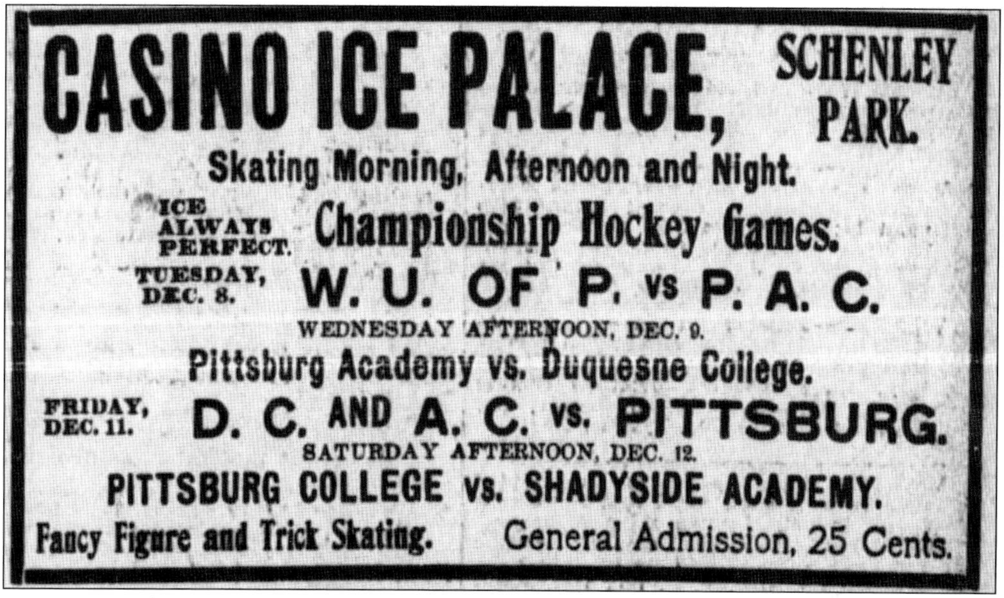

In 1896, two leagues were formed: an interscholastic league for high schools and the Western Pennsylvania Hockey League (WPHL) for adults. WPHL teams were the Pittsburgh Athletic Club (PAC), Duquesne Country and Athletic Club (DC&AC), Western University of Pennsylvania (WUP, now University of Pittsburgh), and the casino team. On November 17, 1896, Duquesne defeated the PAC 2-1 in the league's first game. (*Press*).

VIEW OF THE CASINO RUINS.

The casino's life was astonishingly short. Just 18 months after it opened, on December 17, 1896, at 2:15 a.m., a fire began in the pumping room when ammonia began leaking. Two hours later, the main ammonia storage tank exploded with catastrophic results. The intense fire fully consumed the building, all the WPHL teams' hockey equipment, and the new merry-go-round. The adjacent wooden bridge was damaged. Insurance was not adequate to cover the loss. (*Press.*)

Civic leaders immediately began searching for a replacement. Some wanted to rebuild on the same site, but some wanted to add the land to Schenley Park. A trolley barn built in 1890 near the corner of Fifth Avenue and Craig Street in Oakland lacked the grace and style of the casino, but it was nearby and convenient to major trolley lines. A large tree in front would be removed to create a grand portico entrance for the new arena. (PHN.)

Another view of the trolley barn includes a trolley and tracks. The two-story front section provided room on the second floor to convert to a ballroom that could hold dances, theater shows, basketball, and boxing events. The car barn section to the rear with its arched windows provided a long and wide expanse under roof. (CLP.)

FIG. 3.—INTERIOR OF CAR BARN—DUQUESNE TRACTION CO.

The greatest advantage of the car barn was that it provided a large clear expanse that could hold an ice rink and enough height to create seating for spectators. Here, the roof trusses and skylights are visible. Pits in the floor provided access to the undercarriage of the trolleys. (PHN.)

Political boss Christopher Lyman Magee spent $500,000 to purchase and renovate the carbarn into a multiuse entertainment venue that would host rodeos, boxing, theater, and movies, as well as an ice rink. It opened on January 23, 1899, with over 10,000 attending. The tree in front has been removed and replaced by the Victorian-style entrance portico. A rooftop sign is partially visible proclaiming the new name, Duquesne Garden. (CLP.)

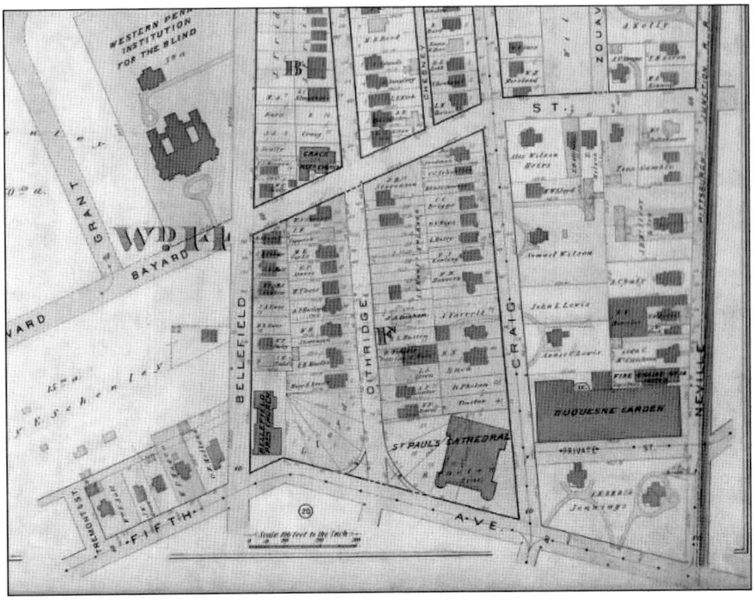

This 1904 Hopkins insurance map places the venue in its neighborhood context. Across Craig Street is St. Paul's Cathedral, then under construction and set to open in 1906. City Fire Station No. 14 is located adjacent to the rear of Duquesne Garden. The Oakland civic center was growing rapidly, including Forbes Field opening a few blocks south in 1909. (UP.)

This view of the facade from June 1900 shows advertising posters for *The Mikado*, including two signboards flanking the entrance to the portico. In the summer, "the Garden" presented weekly light operas in the main hall. A portion of the main floor was converted to a palm garden with potted greenery, café tables, light refreshments, and concerts. (PHN.)

The WPHL was revived with the first game on January 24, 1899. In this January 17, 1900, photograph, roof trusses, lighting, and seating areas are visible. Cross ties have been added to the base of the trusses. Skylights have been blacked out. The front row of seats is about five feet above the ice. A "running board" at the base of the wall encircles the ice. The ice was 50 feet longer than a modern NHL rink. (PHN.)

While its artificial ice rink was its most unique asset, Duquesne Garden was always a multipurpose venue. The hall was built with a stage at the Neville Street end of the building. Ice could be removed and seating for 1,200 brought in. Here, the hall is set for a stage performance. (PHN.)

A bustling Wednesday afternoon in 1902 with carriages arriving for the matinee is evidence of Duquesne Garden's popularity. In addition to summer stage and concert performances in the main hall, the second floor housed a ballroom that was popular for dances, parties, and charity events. The elaborate original portico entrance is clearly visible here, along with a police officer in a "bobby"-style helmet. (*Bulletin.*)

Another view from 1902 shows the portico with a nameplate, cast-iron columns set on stone bases, decorative details, and electric lights. The well-dressed crowd includes many women in their finery. Compare this image with views of the Art Deco marquee from the 1950s and one can see the same support columns. (*Bulletin.*)

On January 19, 1901, the PAC took on the visiting Queens University team before 5,523 spectators. Though the PAC lost 1-0, the public interest in hockey was clear. Note the arched windows on the side walls and the running board encircling the ice. At this early date, there is no mezzanine. (CLP.)

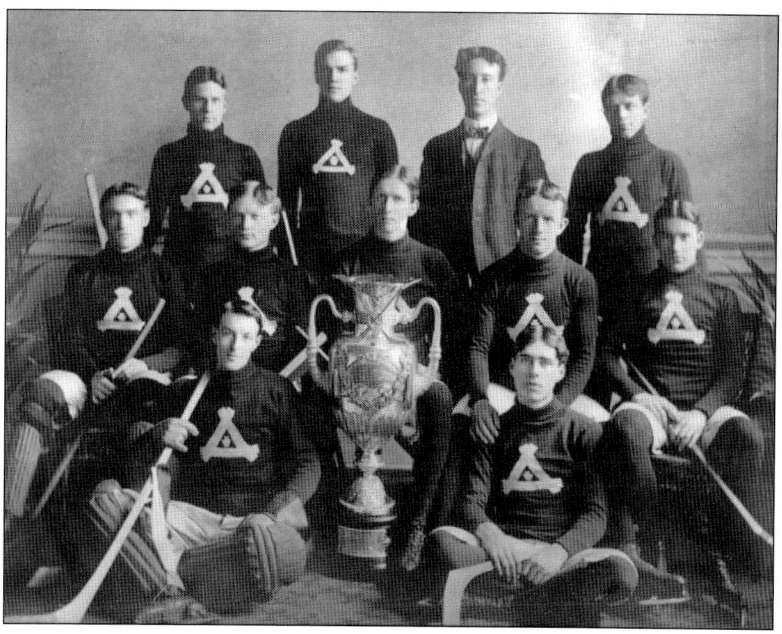

The 1901 PAC team poses with its magnificent trophy. The 1901–1902 season of the WPHL opened with three teams: Keystones, Bankers, and PAC. The league was ostensibly amateur, but in reality, players were being paid or given no-show jobs, giving Pittsburgh a claim as the birthplace of professional hockey. (PHN.)

This postcard view of the facade includes a good crowd and a trolley. By 1902, the WPHL was openly pro and attracting top talent from Canada. Because of its size, quality, and extended season, the rink itself was a major factor in attracting talented players. Pittsburgh had become the hot spot for professional hockey. (AC.)

In 1904–1905, the best of the WPHL teams were combined to create the Pittsburgh Pros in the International Professional Hockey League (IPHL), the first intercity and fully professional league. The 1906–1907 Pros, shown here, finished third in the five-team league. By this time, professional leagues were popping up in Canada, so Canadian players soon found opportunities closer to home. The IPHL folded at the end of the 1906–1907 season. (*Post.*)

The WPHL was revived for 1907–1908 with original members Pittsburgh Athletic Club and the Bankers (note dollar sign logos) and new members Pittsburgh Lyceum and Pittsburgh Pirates, the latter headed by baseball club owner Barney Dreyfuss. With Duquesne Garden's artificial ice, the league started its season before the various Canadian leagues, still dependent on natural ice, but as winter deepened, Canadian players abandoned the WPHL to return north. The league folded after the 1908–1909 season. (AC.)

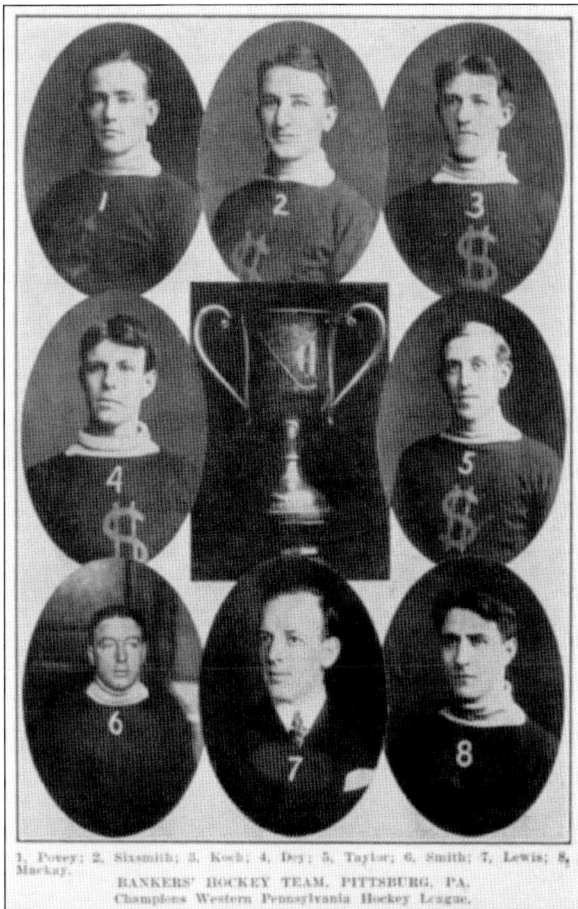

Hockey returned to the Garden in 1915 when local politician Roy Schooley became its manager and founded the Duquesne Garden amateur team, sometimes known as the Yellow Jackets. Here, the Garden is decked out with fabric covering the roof trusses for a 1916 championship series against St. Paul. The arched windows are visible, and the running boards still encircle the ice. (HG.)

The 1916 champions pose in front of an orchestra on the Garden's theater stage. In 1916, they swept a three-game series from the St. Paul Saints and claimed the national amateur championship. In 1916–1917, the team affiliated with the Pittsburgh Athletic Association (PAA), not to be confused with the earlier Pittsburgh Athletic Club (PAC). The team adopted the PAA's "winged head" logo and compiled a 37-3-0 record. (PHN.)

The 1916–1917 PAA team poses in their "winged head" uniforms. In 1917–1918, the team joined the US National Hockey League and won the championship in the league's only season. Wartime restrictions on ammonia and the loss of many players to military service closed most rinks in 1918. Duquesne Garden was leased to serve as a military barracks. In 1919–1920, the PAA team resumed play at Duquesne Garden as an independent club, going 25-5-3. (AC.)

Hockey's Olympic debut came in the 1920 Winter Games in Antwerp, Belgium. Top amateur clubs played to determine the best US team, but player eligibility issues forced the assembly of a new club. It fell to Roy Schooley (first row, center) to organize the first US Olympic hockey team. The Garden hosted tryouts, and Schooley's new team played exhibition games at the Garden to raise funds and hone its game. The team won silver in Antwerp. (LOC.)

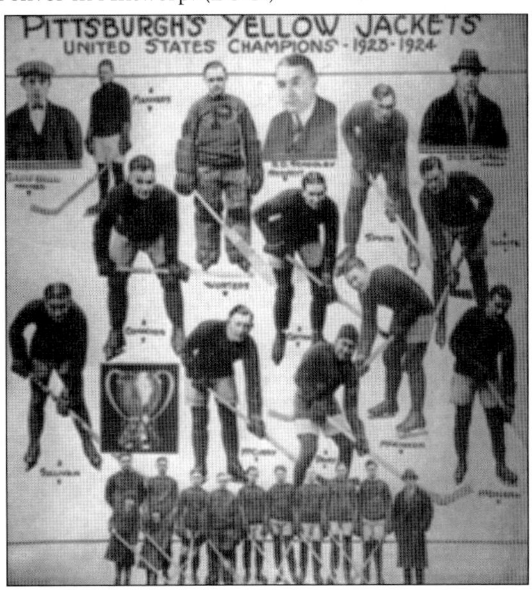

In 1920, Schooley helped found the US Amateur Hockey Association (USAHA) with the PAA team as a member. By 1922–1923, the PAA team became the Pittsburgh Yellow Jackets and donned black-and-gold uniforms, beginning Pittsburgh's association with those colors for sports teams. They won the USAHA championship the following two seasons. Ostensibly "amateurs," the team attracted star players from Canada for more than a hearty pat on the back. (AC.)

In 1924–1925, the Yellow Jackets had enough players to field another club, the Fort Pitt Hornets. Both teams played at the Garden as members of the USAHA but in separate divisions. Each team won its division and met for the championship. The Jackets took the title series 3-0-1. The USAHA folded after the 1924–1925 season, and the Yellow Jackets and Hornets ceased operations. (*Post-Gazette.*)

Just as the USAHA was folding in 1925, Duquesne Garden was awarded a franchise in the new National Hockey League (NHL). To meet NHL standards, the massive Garden rink was shortened by 50 feet. Though unrelated to the baseball team, the hockey team was named the Pittsburgh Pirates. It signed many former Yellow Jackets and played the first NHL game in Pittsburgh on December 2, 1925, a 2-1 win over the New York Americans. (BL.)

This artist's sketch from a 1925 program cover shows the interior with fabric draped on the ceiling to cover the roof trusses. Elaborate fixtures light the ice. The original seating and arched windows are still visible, and there is no mezzanine. (PHN.)

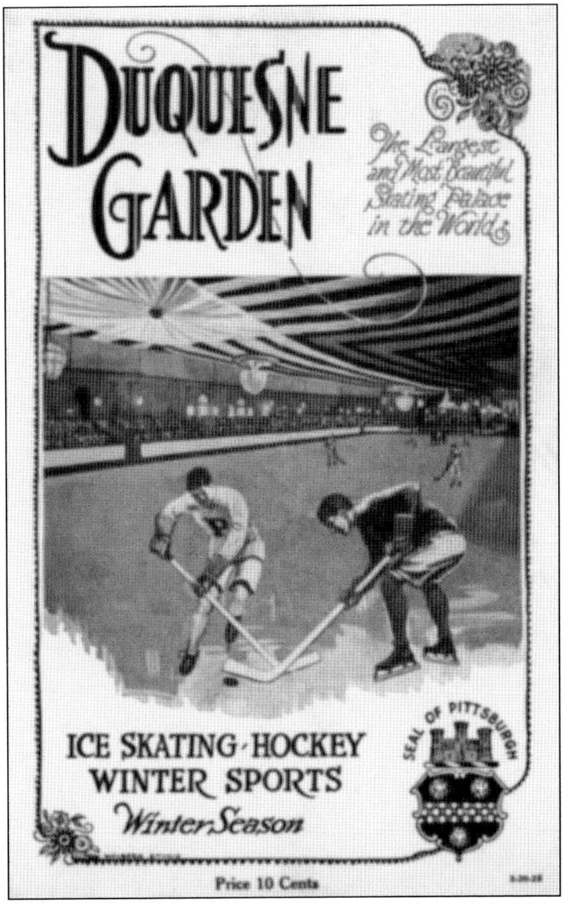

In this undated view, the arched windows have been covered over, and mezzanines have been added. The date of these changes is unclear, but Duquesne Garden management was ousted in 1923 by unhappy creditors. Schooley headed a new management group and made extensive renovations in 1923 and 1924. Soon, the group would buy the building from the Duquesne Traction Company for $360,000. (*Press*.)

Duquesne Garden was a multipurpose venue, hosting trade shows, political meetings, theatrical shows, dances, amateur sports, and even a dance marathon. This 1926 radio show featured the hot new technology. It was held on the main floor with the ice removed. The dasher boards, mezzanine, and seating are visible. (*Press.*)

Henry Townsend, Political Leader, Dies in Hospital

City Property Superintendent Succumbs After Emergency Operation.

Henry Townsend, aged 55, superintendent of city property, active business man and a promoter of indoor athletics, died at St. Francis Hospital yesterday morning following a two days' illness of influenza. Complications had necessitated an emergency operation for which Mr. Townsend was taken to the hospital Friday midnight. He was unable to overcome subsequent developments.

The death of Mr. Townsend came as a surprise, as it was not known that he was seriously ill. He had

POLITICAL LEADER DIES

Henry Townsend.

Henry Townsend was a prominent politician and president of Duquesne Garden Arena Co. with plans to dramatically remake the interior to increase capacity from 6,000 to 12,000. On January 16, 1927, Townsend died unexpectedly at the age of 55 after a bout of influenza and emergency surgery. His son Horace took over management but never fully implemented his father's expansion plan, leaving Duquesne Garden with the smallest seating capacity in the NHL. (*Press.*)

Duquesne Garden dodged disaster several times. A 1920 fire destroyed dressing rooms. A 1926 fire in the roof caused $30,000 in damage. On July 25, 1928, a valve on an ammonia storage tank failed and released a poisonous cloud into Oakland. The Garden's engineer, a nearby resident, and several firefighters were overcome by the fumes but recovered. Here, firefighters use respirators rushed over from the Bureau of Mines a few blocks away. (*Press.*)

In 1928, retired boxer Benny Leonard (standing right) bought the NHL Pirates from Horace Townsend and leased the Garden for home games. The Pirates struggled for two losing seasons with low attendance, even moving late-season home games to other cities to cut financial losses. Duquesne Garden was described as "drab and dirty" and unprofitable for teams. After the 1929–1930 season, the team moved to Philadelphia as the Quakers, but it folded after one season. (HG.)

With the NHL Pirates gone, Schooley revived the Yellow Jackets in 1930 by acquiring a franchise in the International Hockey League (IHL). Arena management also tried bringing boxing back, but troubles multiplied. The city moved to collect $46,000 in unpaid taxes. The mortgage holder forced a sheriff's sale. Schooley faced indictment for corruption, then took ill, was bedridden, and died. At the end of the 1931–1932 season, the Yellow Jackets' lease was cancelled. (*Sun-Telegraph.*)

The year 1932 boiled with rumors and confusion. Art Rooney tried to buy the IHL franchise and then tried to team with New York gangster Big Bill Dwyer to buy the NHL Pirates. Ultimately, the NHL refused to approve the Pirates sale, the IHL canceled the Yellow Jackets franchise, and a frustrated Rooney said, "I'm through with hockey." Pittsburgh was without professional hockey, but a year later, Rooney obtained an NFL football franchise. (*Press.*)

Everyone acknowledged that the small, antiquated arena was a problem. Benny Leonard had proposed building a new \$1.5-million venue. Schooley had proposed \$100,000 in improvements. Rooney's group planned a rebuild of the interior to increase seating. Civic leaders considered sites for a new "Town Hall" sports and entertainment venue, including the Garden site as shown here. Nothing happened. (*Press.*)

This low aerial view shows St. Paul Cathedral with the arched roof of the Garden partially visible beyond the church. The Victorian mansion alongside the Garden is the E.H. Jennings House, but billboards have encroached onto the grounds of the estate, and the grand house was eventually demolished. (CMOA.)

On March 1, 1932, a fire broke through the Garden roof while 125 children were skating inside. The children evacuated, and firefighters climbed to the roof to contain the blaze with moderate damage. Central Catholic High School is in the background. In December 1932, theater entrepreneur John H. Harris and Harris Enterprises took over management of the aging venue, and the future began to brighten. (*Sun-Telegraph.*)

A rare view shows the concession stand at Duquesne Garden, where skaters and event patrons could have a cool drink and a bite. Harris began to make upgrades and much-needed repairs in the aging facility. (*Sun-Telegraph.*)

In 1935, the Yellow Jackets were again revived by John H. Harris, this time as a new franchise in the Eastern Amateur Hockey League (EAHL). This 1935 photograph shows the team in the Garden locker room, which can best be described as utilitarian, with just a shelf for liniments and tape and a few hooks for coats and hats. (PHN.)

In 1935, longtime hockey promoter Larry Welch obtained a franchise in the professional IHL and dubbed them the Shamrocks. The Yellow Jackets and Shamrocks both used the Garden as home ice, but neither found success. The 1935–1936 Shamrocks lost $40,000 in four months and folded after their only season, with the final game canceled due to the devastating 1936 St. Patrick's Day flood. (PHN.)

A group shot of the 1936 Yellow Jackets on the bench offers a close view of the rink's seating. Note the vertical wainscoting at the front and rear of the seating section and the "No Smoking" signs posted on the wall. The dasher boards show considerable wear. The amateur Yellow Jackets outlived the professional Shamrocks, but not by much. After the 1936–1937 season, the Yellow Jackets folded. (PHN.)

Pittsburgh was not done with professional hockey. In 1936, after the death of the Shamrocks, John Harris acquired the IHL champion Detroit Olympics and moved them to Duquesne Garden, where they became the Pittsburgh Hornets of the International-American League (later renamed the American Hockey League). Finally, the Hornets were a franchise with staying power, remaining until the Garden's closure in 1956. Here, one can see the protective mesh screen atop the dasher boards behind the players. (*Sun-Telegraph.*)

The Garden seated somewhat more than 5,000 spectators, making it one of the smallest venues in professional hockey. Overflow crowds were permitted upon approval of the city fire marshal, located in the firehouse next to the rear of the arena. Some nights, 7,000 to 8,000 fans would pack the 5,000-seat venue. (PHN.)

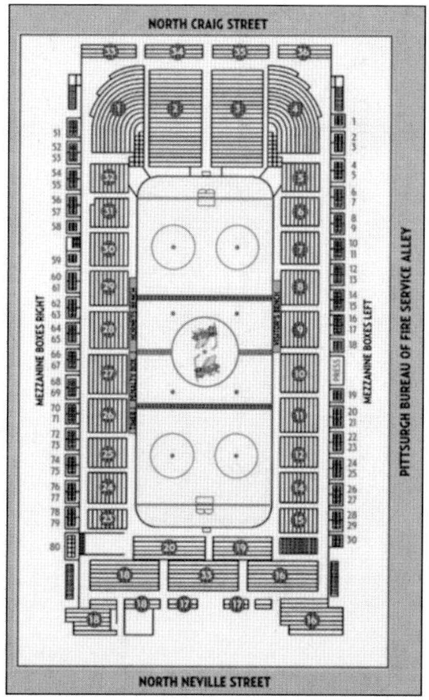

With its antiquated ice-making system, converting the arena's surface for different events was problematic. Freezing ice for hockey could take several days. Waiting for it to melt took even longer, so the ice was broken up and shoveled out, as seen in this rare news photograph. (*Sun-Telegraph.*)

In 1935, the versatile Garden began hosting annual international cycling races with a banked hardwood track, but more notable here is the Iron City Beer hockey scoreboard in the background. Management also spared no expense here in decorating with bunting and flags. (PHN.)

Skating as recreation remained popular with Pittsburghers, and the Garden regularly held public skating nights from November to April. This 1936 photograph shows a good-sized crowd enjoying the ice. The folding stadium seats are clearly visible. The mezzanine level is visible with a sign on the front edge promoting advertising. (PHN.)

To this point, rinks were surrounded by a mesh screen atop the dasher boards to protect fans from flying pucks, sticks, and players. In 1938, Pittsburgh Plate Glass (PPG) introduced a shatter-resistant tempered glass called Herculite. With its headquarters in Pittsburgh, the company naturally turned to the local hockey team to test the new material. (HHC.)

With successful tests of PPG's Herculite, in 1940, the Garden became the first arena to install glass above the dasher boards, replacing the old mesh screen. This soon became standard for professional leagues. Although other materials have since replaced Herculite in arenas, the glass is still made for doors and windows. (HHC.)

Fans did not have to travel to Oakland to get tickets. This 1939 view shows the Harris Company's Downtown ticket office at Sixth Avenue and Wood Street and its less-than-subtle signage. Events listed include hockey, boxing, Ice Follies, and more. (*Sun-Telegraph*.)

In 1942, the Arena Managers Association (AMA), with John H. Harris as president, purchased 10 new Bulova scoreboards for hockey arenas, including Duquesne Garden. Clocks counted down game time and penalty time, as well as providing the score. (Recker.)

The 1945–1946 Hornets pose on the ice at Duquesne Garden. The scoreboard includes ads for Duquesne Pilsener flanking the clock. The seating extends high up the back wall. At the far right are large letters identifying the venue as Duquesne Garden. (PHN.)

On March 31, 1936, Garden manager John H. Harris hired skating sensation Sonja Henie to perform before a Yellow Jackets game. The public response was extraordinary. In 1940, the Arena Managers Association, representing nine major arenas including the Garden, met in Hershey, Pennsylvania, and created a touring ice show titled Ice Capades. It ran for 57 years, until 1997. This interior view with bunting in the rafters is from the 1951 *Skating Annual* magazine. (Recker.)

John Harris was always open to new ideas. In the early 1950s, he bought one of the first Zamboni ice resurfacers for the Garden and another (now in the Hockey Hall of Fame) to travel with the Ice Capades. Here, inventor Frank Zamboni sits in the driver's seat of a Model B at an unidentified rink. The early Zambonis were built on a Jeep body, so standing with Frank is his lucky local Jeep dealer. (Zamboni.)

In January 1940, Harris announced a name change—to The Gardens. Motor Square Garden had closed its competing boxing venue, and "Gardens" was easier to fit in ads and headlines. The grand Victorian-era portico was given an Art Deco makeover for a more modern marquee, but the support posts are original to the 1899 version. The events listed on the marquee illustrate the wide variety of attractions at The Gardens. (HHC.)

This is a close-up view of the marquee and its bright lights, an inviting beacon on this Oakland street. As always, The Gardens had a busy schedule with a New Year's Eve party, basketball, and hockey. (HHC.)

With expiration of the Harris Company's lease and redevelopment plans for the site, The Gardens closed in the spring of 1956. The last event was a Hornets 3-2 triple-overtime loss to the Cleveland Barons on April 3, 1956, in the Calder Cup semifinals. Without a home venue, the Hornets franchise went on hiatus until the opening of the Civic Arena in 1961. Here the marquee simply announces "Closed for Events." (AC.)

The Gardens is seen in its final days, with peeling paint, broken windows, and empty sidewalks. Over 58 years, it had been the cradle of professional hockey, the birthplace of US Olympic hockey and the Ice Capades, the site of the first NHL and NBA games in Pittsburgh, home to NIT champion Duquesne University basketball and Calder Cup champion AHL hockey teams, and a boxing ring for Joe Louis, Billy Conn, Fritzie Zivic, and Harry Greb. (*Post-Gazette.*)

Demolition began on August 13, 1956. Here, the famed marquee comes down. In addition to sporting events, The Gardens' marquee held the names of dozens of performers, including Enrico Caruso, Jelly Roll Morton, Cab Calloway, and Roy Rogers and Trigger. Duquesne Garden certainly fulfilled its original goal of being a multipurpose venue. (HHC.)

In this interior view during the dismantling of The Gardens, seats have been removed, exposing the terraced floor. Herculite glass panels atop the dashers have been removed. Scaffolding has been erected on the ice to facilitate the removal of fixtures. (PHN.)

Demolition of the structure exposed roof trusses, the proscenium arch of the stage, and details of the seating sections. Once the site was cleared, the Plaza Park Apartments and a Stouffers Restaurant were built. In 1979, Stouffers became Duranti's. Both included a brick wall from The Gardens. It was salvaged by Jim Kubus of pittsburghhockey.net and later reinstalled at Consol Center (now PPG Paints Arena). Visible at the far left is the city fire station. (*Post-Gazette.*)

Exposition Buildings became popular in the late 1800s as a combination convention center, trade show, and cultural attraction. Pittsburgh's first was located in Allegheny City. It was destroyed by fire in 1883 but gave its name to the ballpark built on its grounds. A new Exposition Hall, seen here, was built near the Point in 1889 on a 50-year lease from the city. On St. Patrick's Day 1901, it too was destroyed by fire. (UP.)

Pittsburgh's third attempt at an Exposition Building cost $600,000 and was erected on the same site near the Point. It consisted of three buildings: the Music Hall (center, with scaffolding still in place on the facade), the Main Hall (right), and Machinery Hall (distant far right). Annual expositions were popular until 1910, when attendance began fading. The last exposition was held in 1916. (LOC.)

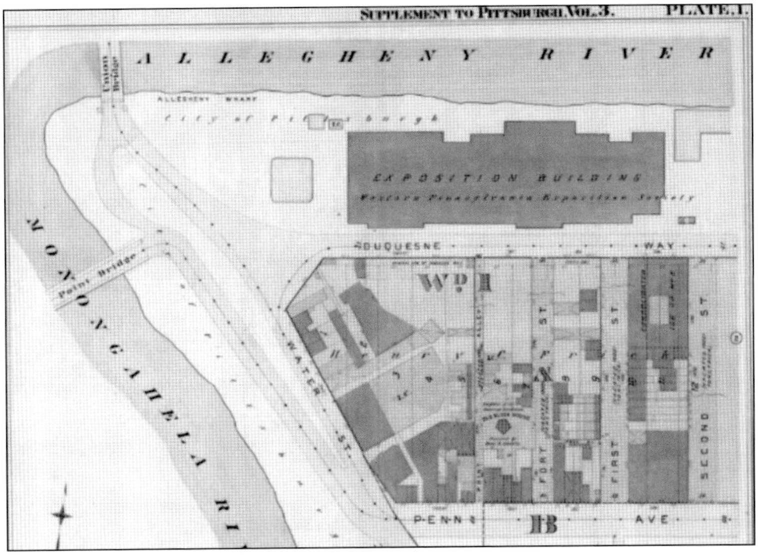

The reconstructed Exposition Buildings are shown in this 1903 Hopkins insurance map along with the other structures at the Point. The Fort Pitt Blockhouse, Pittsburgh's oldest building, is a short distance south of the Exposition Buildings. (UP.)

The arched windows of the Main Hall are seen at the end of this sad little street. The Exposition Buildings were a grand architectural statement in the midst of railroad tracks, industrial buildings, and ramshackle housing. Nonetheless, it was a popular destination for both Pittsburgh residents and visitors and a major source of civic pride. (HHC.)

This panorama of the Point during the 1907 flood shows the devastation regularly caused by the rivers. Downtown and the lower wards of the city of Allegheny (now the North Shore) were most affected. Despite public outcry and tremendous damage to property, flood controls were not

implemented until after the Great St. Patrick's Day Flood of 1936, the city's most devastating. The Music Hall facade rises above the train sheds at far left. The banks of the rivers and the Point are obliterated by the water. A rowboat full of people is at left center. (LOC.)

The monumental classical design of the facade is seen here with the Music Hall entrance (left) and the Main Hall (right). Distant at far right is a tower of Machinery Hall. The Music Hall seated over 5,000 patrons and hosted all the great bands and orchestras of the early 20th century. The Main Hall continued to host annual expositions until World War I and the Spanish flu epidemic brought an end to such gatherings. (UP.)

Another major attraction at the expositions was a figure-8 roller coaster, seen here from across the Allegheny River. The west side of the Music Hall is at left. The Manchester Bridge is under construction at right. It would open in 1915 and last until 1970. (UP.)

This 1916 view of the Point shows the Exposition Buildings at right, now partially obscured by the freight house of the Pennsylvania Railroad. The coaster is visible at center. Exposition Park, home of the Pirates before the construction of Forbes Field, is across the river, and the Manchester and Point Bridges are at left. (UP.)

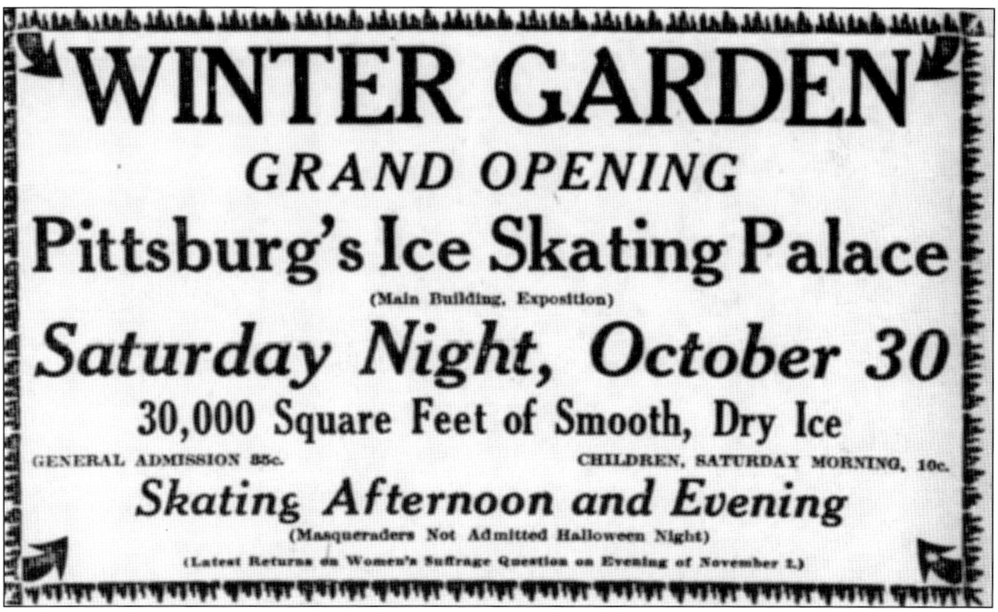

Declining attendance at expositions, the growing popularity of skating, and the high demand for ice time at Duquesne Garden prompted the exposition board to add an ice rink in the Main Hall in 1915. State-of-the-art refrigeration equipment was located in Machinery Hall, and a brine solution was pumped through pipes beneath a new concrete floor in the Main Hall. Dubbed the "Winter Garden," its advertised opening was delayed a week. (*Post.*)

In 1916, Winter Garden management hired Arthur Sixsmith, one of the first professional hockey players, to recruit players for a Winter Garden team. Originally from Ottawa, Sixsmith came to Pittsburgh to play professionally at Duquesne Garden. For two seasons, he captained the Pittsburgh Pros in the first fully professional league. After his playing days, he stayed in Pittsburgh and began a banking career, eventually becoming Andrew W. Mellon's personal assistant. (*Press.*)

The Winter Garden team was formed to play games against local and visiting teams, giving the venue an additional attraction, but the team played only four games, losing three. After that one short season, the team folded. Shown here is defenseman C.M. Young. (*Press.*)

For 1916–1917, Winter Garden management hit upon a novel idea: women's hockey. Three teams were formed: Winter Garden Girls, Polar Maids, and Arctic Maids. They constituted one of the first women's leagues. The experiment lasted just that one season. (*Press.*)

WOMEN'S TEAMS TO PLAY HOCKEY AT WINTER GARDEN

THE WINTER GARDEN GIRLS' HOCKEY TEAM.

On March 24, 1917, Hobey Baker led a Philadelphia amateur team against Pittsburgh's best amateurs at the Winter Garden. One of hockey's first great stars, he scored all three goals in Philadelphia's 3-2 overtime win. It was his last game. After gallant service as a fighter pilot in World War I, he died in a crash on the day he was to return to the States. He was inducted into the Hockey Hall of Fame. (AC.)

Due to war and influenza, no hockey was played at the Winter Garden in 1917–1918. In 1919, the exposition board closed the facility and relinquished its lease to the city, which then used the property for an auto pound and storage. The Music Hall was demolished in 1941 and is gone at far left in this 1943 view of the Main Hall. Machinery Hall was razed in 1942, and its steel was given to the war effort. (UP.)

The Main Hall, which briefly hosted early hockey teams, was the last exposition building to meet the wrecking ball. This 1951 photograph shows the steel structure that created the wide clear span that accommodated an ice rink and seating. In the background, its grand arched windows are still visible. The site is now part of Point State Park. (UP.)

Four

Modern Hockey Arenas

Despite being small and antiquated, Duquesne Garden was the only viable venue for professional hockey in the region after the demise of the Winter Garden. When it closed abruptly in 1956, there was no alternative. The development of a replacement venue would take a long and torturous path.

Interest in developing a new arena first arose in the 1920s, when Duquesne Garden was already seen as antiquated and too small compared to arenas in other comparable cities. Sites ranging from Oakland to East Liberty's Motor Square Garden were considered but never advanced.

Civic leaders headed by department store mogul Edgar Kaufmann again began thinking about a new multipurpose facility near the end of World War II. Frank Lloyd Wright, who had designed Fallingwater for Kaufmann, was given the first crack at designing a new multiuse civic center to include a sports arena, theaters, cultural facilities, offices, and parking. The Point was the chosen site. Wright's concept was immense in size, ambition, and cost. It was rejected by civic leaders as impractical. A second scheme was equally grandiose, and Wright's involvement ended.

Two separate concepts proceeded on parallel tracks. Kaufmann and city councilman Abe Wolk championed a new facility for the Civic Light Opera, which was using Pitt Stadium for its shows where the open air subjected the company and the audience to the vagaries of the weather. Mayor David Lawrence and other leaders wanted a multiuse facility that would provide for indoor sports, conventions, trade shows, and cultural performances. Initially, the only thing the two concepts had in common was a movable roof. Eventually, these two concepts coalesced into one, commonly referred to as the Civic Auditorium.

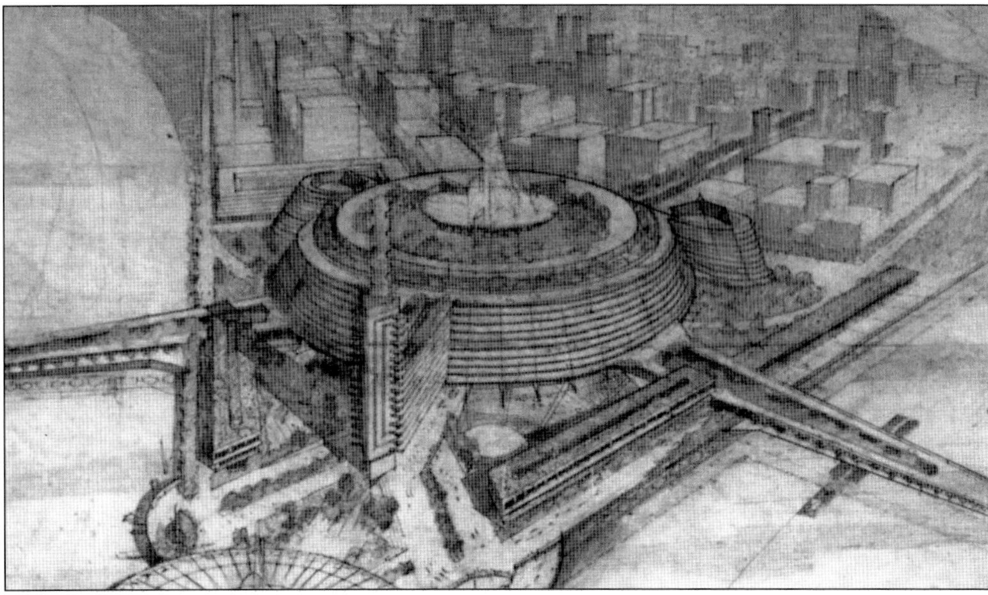

Wright's first scheme included a massive circular building with a cantilevered roadway spiraling around its exterior, somewhat like the spiral ramps of the Guggenheim Museum but for cars. At the Point was another circular structure that housed a pool, an aquarium, and a restaurant. (PA.)

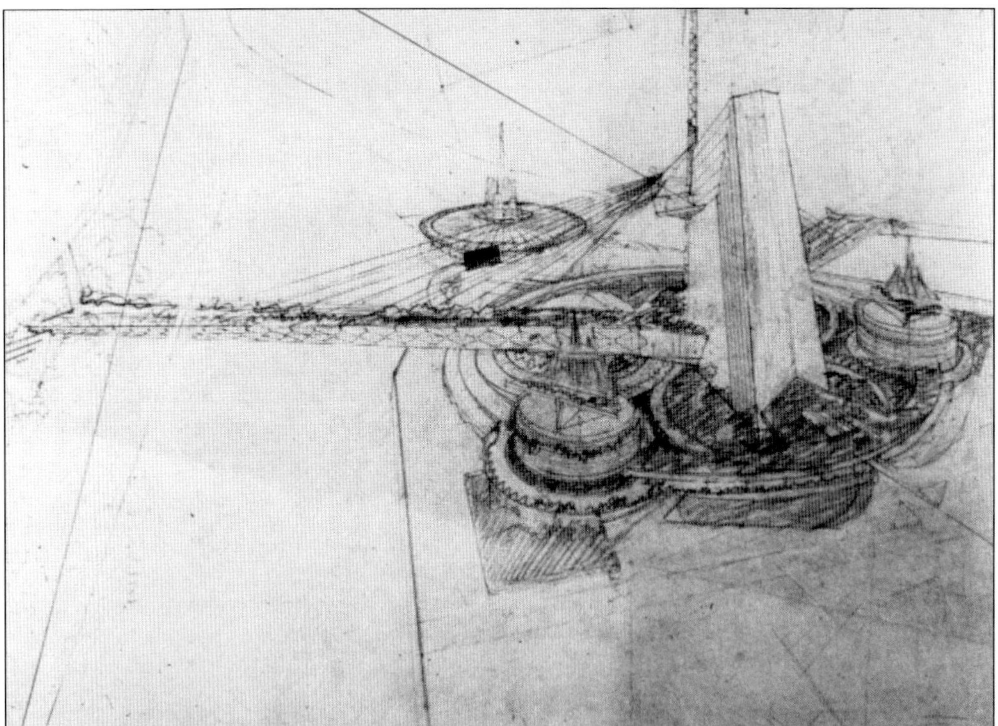

Wright's second concept was just as outrageous as the first. A mammoth central tower replaced the circular building with new bridges crossing the Monongahela and the Allegheny. A Pittsburgh delegation traveled to Wright's Taliesin West studio on January 4, 1948, for a presentation by Wright, but the new plan received no more support than the first. (PA.)

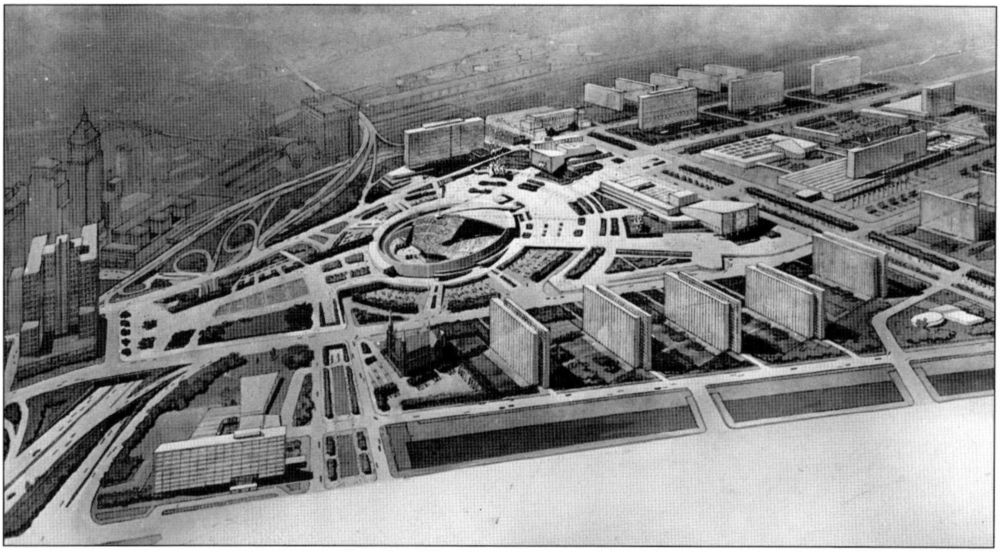

The attention of civic leaders shifted to the Lower Hill, which was viewed as dense and blighted, with a high concentration of substandard buildings, unsanitary conditions, and disease. It was also the economic and social heart of the African American community, but that was apparently of little concern to the all-white civic leadership. This 1953 concept drawing shows the development area extending deep into the Hill with a line of monolithic apartment buildings. (CLP.)

Civic leaders view a model of the planned new home of the Civic Light Opera, which at this early design phase had an innovative folding fabric roof. Philanthropist Edgar Kaufmann (left) and Councilman Abe Wolk (second from left) were instrumental in pushing the project forward. Kaufmann passed away before the opening of the Civic Arena, but Wolk lived to 91 and saw the Civic Arena become a reality. (PHN.)

Here is the Lower Hill prior to clearing land for redevelopment. Bigelow Boulevard marks the left edge, while Bedford, Wylie, and Centre Avenues form the east-west spine of the Hill. In the far distant top right is the Cathedral of Learning in Oakland. (CLP.)

Rather than working to strengthen the community, city leadership's solution was to obliterate it and start over, to create a dramatic modern civic center that would redefine Pittsburgh's image and reputation. This aerial gives a sense of the scale of the project area, more than 100 acres. Bigelow Boulevard is at the bottom, and Centre Avenue runs diagonally at top. (CLP.)

After a lengthy design process, the concept for the arena and the surrounding complex gelled, as depicted in this 1956 planning model. A fabric roof gave way to stainless steel. Construction bids were opened in February 1958. While the plan called for other structures, including a theater, concert hall, and other cultural facilities, ultimately the only structures completed were the arena and one I.M. Pei–designed apartment building. (CLP.)

Mayor David Lawrence and other dignitaries stand inside a dump truck while a large excavator prepares to dig the first shovelful for the Civic Auditorium on April 25, 1958. More than 8,000 residents and 400 businesses were displaced. Demolitions took five years, severely disrupting the remaining community and leaving impacts that still reverberate today. (CMOA.)

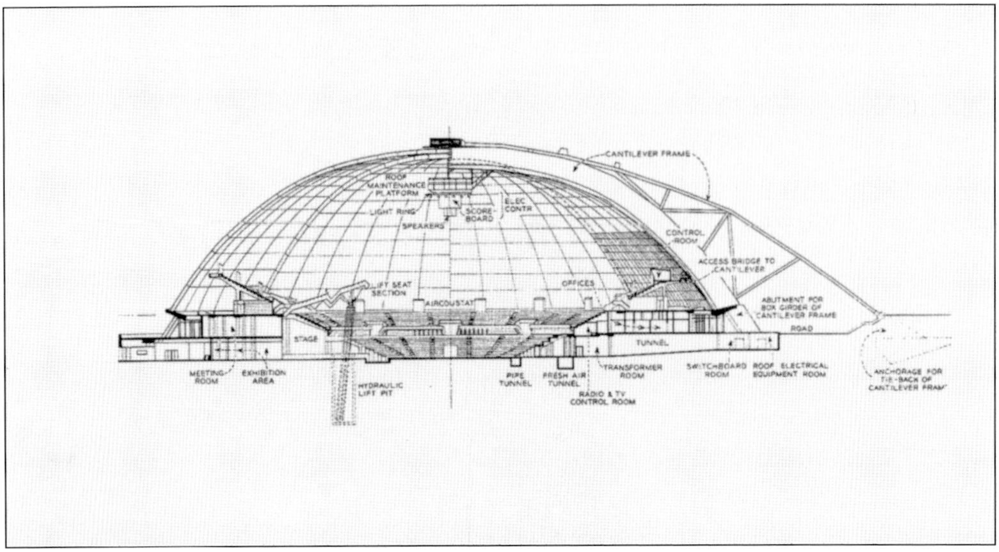

This architectural drawing provides a clear illustration of the arena's various components. Nothing like this had been attempted before, and the arena would be a demonstration of Pittsburgh's talent for design, engineering, and manufacturing. (MRA.)

Construction began with the anchorage for the cantilever arch (top right), which allowed for an unobstructed interior with no internal supports. Here, the perimeter of the building has taken shape, encircling the arena floor and seating bowl. The movable roof panels would roll on this concrete and steel ring. At the bottom right, one can see the angled supports that buttressed the base for the dome. (MRA.)

The steel frame of the shell is taking shape. The cost of the project was $22 million in 1960 dollars ($227 million in 2023). Just beyond the peak of the arena dome in this view is the Melody Tent, the temporary home of the Civic Light Opera from 1959 until it moved into the new arena in 1961. (CLP.)

Once the steel frame was built, the roof had to be insulated and skinned with stainless steel. This view shows workmen on exterior scaffolding. The dome would be skinned in 2,950 tons of stainless steel. (PA.)

A dramatic interior view during construction shows the inside of the dome, which would also be skinned, requiring extensive interior scaffolding. The seating tiers are taking shape in this view. (CLP.)

The dome consisted of eight panels, six of which were movable. These pivoted on a massive hinge at the highest point of the cantilever arm. Again, a structure of this kind had never been attempted before, so the ingenuity of the engineering is still astonishing. (MRA.)

The six movable leaves of the roof rolled on 78 wheels, shown here at the Homestead Steel Works, Wheel and Axle Division, where they were made in 1958. The roof took 2.5 minutes to fully open. (UP.)

With the Civic Arena nearing completion, the Pittsburgh Hornets of the American Hockey League, dormant since the closing of The Gardens, were revived. Here, team business manager Baz Bastien (left) and John McGreevy of Harris Entertainment pose in front of the new arena with improvised hockey sticks. Behind them, the entrance plaza is nearing completion. (CLP.)

This early view of the completed arena shows the original entrance plaza and the newly planted landscaping. There is no marquee on the exterior. Originally dubbed the "Civic Auditorium," it quickly became known as the "Civic Arena" because that was easier to fit on signs. Colloquially, it became "the Igloo." (MRA.)

The new arena was dedicated on September 17, 1961, two and a half years after the start of construction. The dome was partially opened for the ceremonies, which included a performance by the Pittsburgh Symphony. Two days later, the Ice Capades, which began at Duquesne Garden, presented the first public event. Note the first of the arena's three scoreboards suspended from the high point of the cantilever arm. (PA.)

This early view shows the roof fully retracted. As built, seating was contained in three tiers in the bowl for a total capacity of 10,732. The empty lots at the top right became the Washington Plaza apartment building, which opened in 1964. (PA.)

This dramatic view shows the cantilever arm and the fully open roof seen from the south side of the building. It illustrates why the Civic Arena was widely considered a modern wonder and an outstanding architectural and engineering achievement. (PA.)

This view shows the interior as it looked when the arena opened. The original seating bowl did not include the balconies at either end of the rink, which were added much later. The original press box is at right. The recessed lighting accentuates the dome. (MRA.)

Civic Light Opera (CLO) had been a major motivating factor behind the Civic Arena's development, and it made its arena debut on July 17, 1962, with *Flower Drum Song*. Concerts like the jazz festival, seen here with the roof one-sixth open, were also a focus. Theater under the stars sounded like a great idea, but unfortunately, the arena's acoustics were not ideal for musical theater, and CLO moved to Heinz Hall in 1973. (AC.)

The Hornets' 1961–1962 program cover included drawings of the old Duquesne Garden marquee and the Civic Auditorium dome. The novelty of the modern venue was an important attraction for fans. The AHL Hornets played their first game in their new home on October 14, 1961, losing 2-1 to Buffalo before 9,317 fans. The Hornets would struggle mightily in their first two seasons, but they finished strong in 1966–1967. (AC.)

This undated view shows the seating bowl set for hockey and the original center scoreboard. Players are on the ice for pre-game warm-ups. Compared to the 5,000-seat Duquesne Garden, this must have seemed cavernous. With the NHL Penguins due to take over the arena in 1967, the Hornets went out with a bang, winning the 1966–1967 Calder Cup as champions of the AHL. (PHN.)

Although Art Rooney had been thwarted in his effort to acquire an NHL franchise in 1932, he was now instrumental in lobbying NHL owners to award an expansion franchise to Pittsburgh in 1966. With the franchise secured, the arena's capacity had to be increased from 10,700 to 12,500 to meet NHL standards. This expansion did not require any structural changes to the venue. Here, the original 1967–1968 Penguins pose in front of the arena stands. (PHN.)

This 1967 view shows the Penguins in action. Clearly visible are the dasher boards with protective glass and the lower-level seating bowl. The expansion Penguins struggled to attract fans, who were used to winning with the AHL Hornets (CLP.)

This 1969 aerial places the arena in context with the Golden Triangle. The US Steel Building is under construction at left center. It would open in 1971. The construction site of Three Rivers Stadium is at top right; the stadium would open in 1970. (PA.)

The arena hosted tennis, including the Pittsburgh Triangles of World Team Tennis from 1974 to 1976, with a championship in 1975, but this image is included because it provides a clear view of the stands without many people in the seats and with the roof open. This view is before the addition of the upper-level terraces at each end of the rink. (PHN.)

Although the arena was barely a decade old, there was a demand for added seating. Fortunately, construction inside a movable dome has its advantages. Here, a beam is brought in through the open dome during the expansion of seating in 1975. At center are the overlapping leaves of the roof, and visible through the door at right is an angled support beam on the exterior concourse. (CLP.)

In the early 1970s, seating was significantly increased over several years. This culminated with the addition of the terrace level balconies overlooking each end of the rink and luxury boxes along the west side of the structure. Both additions are visible in this aerial view. (Compare with the image on page 105.) This renovation raised seating capacity to over 16,000. (PHN.)

The terrace-level balcony is seen in this view of a concert with the roof open and the city skyline beyond. In 1993, a second terrace would be added above the first terrace at both ends. The arena hosted dozens of major musical performers, including Elvis, Sinatra, the Beatles, and Michael Jackson. (PHN.)

Here the arena is set for a concert in 1986 with lights hung from the inside of the dome. Increasingly, performers and promoters preferred to keep the roof closed for better lighting, acoustics, and protection from wind and weather. Openings became rarer. (*Post-Gazette*.)

The broad outdoor concourse encircled the entire perimeter with the unique angled struts that supported the massive roof. Parking lots surrounded the concourse, placing the arena in a sea of pavement that contributed to the impression of an alien spaceship landed in the city. (PA.)

This is how the entrances and turnstiles looked when the arena opened. An interior concourse provided circulation. Over time, seating was increased, but the concourse and hallways could not be expanded. They became crowded and a great annoyance to fans. (MRA.)

The massive roof was operated from this Westinghouse control panel, seen here just prior to the arena's demolition, looking unchanged from its installation in 1960. Aging machinery and the need to hang lights, speakers, and other equipment from the roof made opening the dome an increasingly impractical undertaking. The roof was last fully opened in 1995 and was permanently closed in 2001. (HABS.)

The roof was fully opened for this 1986 concert. The arena's second scoreboard, installed in 1986, is seen at the top of the dome. On July 4, 1962, comedian Carol Burnett was the first to open the dome for an event, declaring, "Ladies and gentlemen, allow me to present the sky!" The roof was partially opened during demolition in 2012, the last opportunity to see the world's first movable dome in action. (PA.)

Mellon Financial Corporation purchased the naming rights in 1999, and the facility was rechristened "Mellon Arena." The front entry plaza was also renovated, adding this marquee with an electronic message board. (HABS.)

This view from Downtown shows the remodeled entrance plaza with the Mellon Arena marquee out front. The Pens won the Stanley Cup in 2009 and entertained fans with a broadcast of the games on outdoor screens erected on the plaza. (PA.)

This view of the Mellon Arena interior includes the third and final scoreboard, a Sony Jumbotron added in 1994. Beyond it are the double terraces behind the goal. These brought the arena's total seating capacity to over 17,000. (PHN.)

This is a view few people ever got—a unique and dizzying view from the peak of the dome under the cantilever arm, looking straight down into the arena. The terrace balconies are at top, and luxury boxes are at either side. (PHN.)

Two famous Pittsburgh domes are pictured; the earlier dome was the portico entry to the Pennsylvania Railroad Station, now the Pennsylvanian apartments and office building. At the time the Civic Arena opened in 1961, it was the largest dome in the world, surpassed three years later by the Houston Astrodome. (PA.)

One last look at the arena's interior is from May 11, 2011, just four months before demolition. The scoreboard has been lowered to the arena floor, and some seats have been dismantled. Several auctions of seats, lockers, signage, and other fragments of the arena raised more than $180,000 for the Sports and Exhibition Authority, and these mementos now decorate man caves throughout Western Pennsylvania. (PA.)

The arena closed for good on June 26, 2010. In September 2011, advocates for the building's preservation gathered to mark the structure's 50th birthday. Despite valiant advocacy efforts and innovative ideas for the reuse of the landmark structure, demolition began just nine days later. (PA.)

The closed arena faces one of its final sunsets with the US Steel Building at left and the Gulf Tower at left center. The arena replaced Duquesne Garden, which was the oldest and smallest NHL hockey arena when it closed in 1956. When the Civic Arena closed in 2010, it was the oldest and third smallest in the NHL. (PA.)

The ceremonial ground-breaking for the new arena was held on August 14, 2008, with the Mellon Arena looming in the background. Construction was completed on August 1, 2010, at a cost of $321 million. Originally named Consol Energy Center, it became PPG Paints Arena in 2016. (PA.)

The structural steel rises quickly in this May 2009 view of construction. Epiphany Church is at left, while the doomed Civic Arena gleams in the distance. A massive five-story banner with stars Evgeni Malkin and Sidney Crosby hangs from the facade. Peeking above the new arena at top right is the I.M. Pei–designed City View, formerly the Washington Plaza Apartments, which opened in 1964. (Hobo Jones.)

An interior view of the construction of the new venue from August 2009 shows the structural underpinnings of the seating bowl. As built, Consol seated approximately 18,000 for hockey and 19,000 for basketball. (PHN.)

Consol is near completion at upper right while the removal of the Igloo's stainless steel has begun. Mellon's naming rights expired soon after the arena closed, so in its final months, it reverted to its traditional name, the Civic Arena. (PHN.)

By January 2012, denuded of its stainless steel, the arena looks rusted and pretty sad. The Penguins retained Wendell August Forge to craft Christmas ornaments from the stainless steel. Forty thousand were made and sold to benefit Penguins team charities. (PHN.)

During demolition, the stationary leaves of the roof remain, along with the luxury boxes at the top of the stands. The last roof panel fell on March 31, 2012. The world's first retractable dome arena lasted a little over 50 years. (PHN.)

Consol Energy Center is seen from the Centre Avenue side in 2010. In the background at left is City View, formerly Washington Plaza Apartments, the last remnant of the original Civic Arena development plan. Consol opened on August 18, 2010, with a Paul McCartney concert. The first Penguins game was a preseason game on September 22, and the first regular season game was a 3-2 loss to the Flyers on October 10. (Doug Kerr.)

This view shows the interior of Consol prior to the first NHL playoff game on April 13, 2011. The Pens would defeat the Tampa Bay Lightning that night 3-0 but lose the series in seven games. In the off-season, 300 seats were added to bring capacity to 18,387, symbolic of star Sidney Crosby's No. 87. The Pens would win the Stanley Cup in 2016 and 2017. (nineteenninety.)

In 2016, PPG Paints bought the naming rights from Consol, as reflected in this 2019 view of the scoreboard. When Consol opened, the goal horn from the Civic Arena was installed at the new facility in a nod to the past. (PA.)

In 2011, the NHL's annual Winter Classic game was played at Heinz Field before a crowd of 68,111. The Pens defeated the Capitals 3-1. Heinz Field also hosted an NHL Stadium Series game in 2017. (PS.)

Five

BASKETBALL VENUES

Like football and hockey, Pittsburgh's professional basketball history dates back to the start of the 20th century. In 1898–1899, Pittsburgh had an amateur league with teams from various sections of the city. By 1902, Manchester and South Side began recruiting and paying top players from other cities.

The Allegheny County Basketball League (ACBL) was formed for the 1903–1904 season. The league was ostensibly amateur, but South Side imported professionals and won the league with a 20-0 record. With such competitive imbalance, the ACBL folded.

For 1906–1907, the Central Basketball League (CBL) was formed as the first openly professional league, with the South Side Germans playing at the market house. Teams attracted top players from Philadelphia and New England, where the game had deeper roots. The league drew well, averaging 1,500 to 2,000 per game, with a peak of 3,000.

The CBL continued through the 1911–1912 season but began to experience financial issues due to the rising cost of player salaries. In 1912, the CBL folded. Uniontown, Johnstown, and Charleroi moved to the Eastern Basketball League (EBL). Other local teams decided to rely on local talent, and the Western Pennsylvania Basketball League (WPBL) was formed as an amateur circuit.

Meanwhile, there were no black professional basketball leagues akin to baseball's Negro Leagues. Black teams were organized as independent amateur or semipro teams and played at a high level against other local teams and travelling clubs.

In the mid-1920s, new pro leagues arose with uneven results. The American Basketball League (ABL) was formed in 1925 without a Pittsburgh team. In 1926, the National Basketball League (NBL) formed and collapsed in one season. A new Central Basketball League (CBL) formed for 1926–1927 with the Pittsburgh Morrys winning the title, but the CBL promptly folded after that one season.

Professional basketball returned to Pittsburgh in 1935, although still cloaked in an amateur fig leaf, when the Midwest Basketball Conference (MBC) was organized with a Pittsburgh team. Pittsburgh would have several more opportunities to host professional basketball and even have occasional success, but none would last.

Built in 1868–1872, "old" city hall was located on Smithfield Street, Downtown. In the 1890s, it was one of the few buildings with a hall large enough to accommodate basketball, and some of Pittsburgh's earliest games were played here. Replaced by the City-County Building in 1915, it hung on as municipal offices until sold to a developer in 1952, when it was demolished. (UP.)

Duquesne Garden installed a basketball court and cage in the second-floor auditorium with 1,500 seats for spectators. Early basketball games were played in a wire-mesh enclosure to protect spectators and to speed up the game. Thus, players were called "cagers." Here, the 1901 Duquesne Country and Athletic Club practices in the cage. (UP.)

CHAMPION D. C. & A. C. BASKETBALL TEAM AT PRACTICE IN THE NEW CAGES AT DUQUESNE GARDEN AUDITORIUM.

Another early home for basketball was the South Side Market House, built in 1893, seen here as it appeared in 1914. The building had a second-floor gymnasium that seated 2,000 and hosted basketball games and boxing events. (UP.)

On February 6, 1915, a fire gutted the market house, destroying its roof and ornamental towers. This photograph from five days after the fire shows little remaining but the exterior walls. It was rebuilt with the second-floor gymnasium. (UP.)

The basketball court was rebuilt after the 1915 fire and is seen here in 1939. Simple bleachers provide seating for spectators. The use of a cage had generally fallen out of favor by 1915 but persisted in some places until the early 1930s. (UP.)

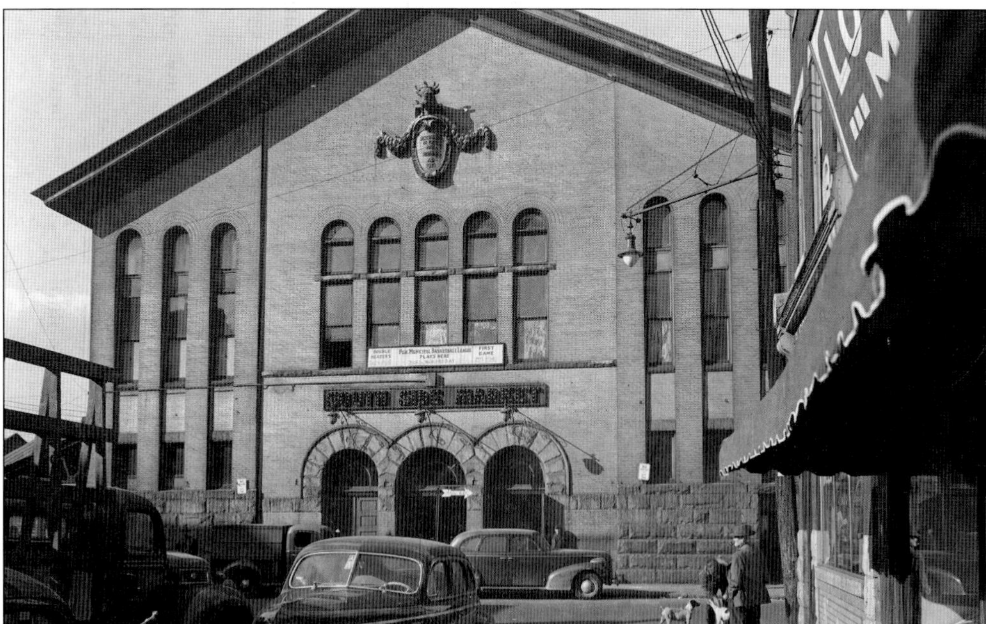

The rebuilt market house is pictured in 1943. Remodeled extensively in 1978 and again in 2011–2012, it remains in use today as a community and recreation center. It is the oldest surviving market house in Pittsburgh and the oldest surviving former professional basketball venue in the city. (UP.)

Like many early teams, the South Side Germans team, captained by Joseph Leithead (second row, left), formed as amateurs at the local YMCA but eventually spun off on their own. This allowed them to play as a semipro team with the South Side Market House as their home base. The 1905–1906 team poses in a studio. Its core players were together for eight successful years. (AC.)

In 1911, Cumberland "Cum" Posey (front row, second from left) coached the Monticello Athletic Association basketball team. Playing against white teams, they established their local dominance. Emboldened by success, they challenged the Howard University team that had gone undefeated in 1911 and had been crowned "Colored Basketball's World Champions." (HHC.)

Monticello practiced and played their home games in the field house at Phipps Playground, mostly because one of the players worked there and had keys to the building. The playground was located across the street from Exposition Park in the city of Allegheny, now Pittsburgh's North Side. The field house is visible at bottom center, partially obscured by trees. The ballpark grandstand is at right. (LOC.)

The Howard team received and accepted Monticello's challenge but did not take the local team seriously. The game was played in the Washington Park Field House in Pittsburgh's Hill District, the exterior seen here in 1919. Monticello crushed the overconfident Howard team in a shocking upset. As a result, Monticello was named "Colored Basketball's World Champions" in 1912. The field house would be demolished in the 1950s to clear land for the Civic Arena. (UP.)

With the success of Monticello, other clubs were organized. The Scholastic Athletic Association and its basketball team were formed in 1915. Based in the Hill District, the athletes were recruited from local schools and colleges, thus giving the team its name. One of the best local teams, it was absorbed into the Loendi Big Five, which would dominate black basketball in the early 1920s. (HHC.)

Another prominent team of the era was the Delaney Rifles, also created by Cum Posey. They practiced with and played against Monticello, and eventually, the two teams would merge into the Monticello-Delaney Club. Later the best local black players would be absorbed into the Loendi Big Five. (HHC.)

Built in 1902 as the Shriners Temple, this building at Webster Avenue and Washington Street in the Hill became the Union Labor Temple in 1911. The building had a 6,000-seat arena for various events including basketball. The Loendi team was named "Colored Basketball's World Champions" for four straight years beginning in 1920. They would regularly fill the arena for games against other local and traveling teams, both white and black. (AC.)

Loendi's biggest rival was an all-Jewish team known as the Second Story Morrys, named after the team sponsor, a retail apparel store. In 1926–1927, the Central Professional Basketball League was revived, and the Morrys won the title in the league's only season using Duquesne University's gym. The Warren, Ohio, team, unhappy with its compensation, tanked the championship game, fatally injuring the league. Chick Davies, future Duquesne University coach, was a member of the 1922–1923 Morrys. (B5.)

In 1935, Pittsburgh was represented in the ostensibly amateur Midwest Basketball Conference by a team from the Young Men's Hebrew Association (YMHA). They played their home games in the YMHA building on Bellefield Avenue in Oakland, which opened in 1924. YMHA finished second in the MBC in the 1935–1936 season but slumped to last in 1936–1937. (SHHS.)

The YMHA building was purchased by the University of Pittsburgh in 1984 and renamed Bellefield Hall. The YMHA gymnasium was refurbished by Pitt for student use in 2005, seen here in 2009. The YMHA organization moved to Squirrel Hill and became the Jewish Community Center. (crazypaco.)

In 1937–1938, the MBC dropped the amateur fig leaf and restructured as an openly pro league, renamed the National Basketball League. The Pittsburgh team was no longer affiliated with YMHA and was renamed the Pirates, though it had no connection with the baseball team. (*Bulletin*.)

Much like the 1926–1927 Second Story Morrys, the Pirates played home games in the Duquesne University gym. The building still stands, repurposed in recent years as the home of the Rangos School of Health Sciences. The gym had limited seating for spectators, but the Pirates gave fans little reason to attend. (DUA.)

The interior of the Duquesne gym, including its wood entry doors, is seen while a Dukes player practices. The Pirates held their own in the NBL in 1937–1938 but fell to last in 1938–1939 and folded. With war on the horizon, Pittsburgh was without professional basketball until 1944. (CMOA.)

Pro basketball returned to Pittsburgh in 1944–1945 with the Pittsburgh Raiders, a new club in the National Basketball League. The team played its home games in the Duquesne University Gym, which had its seating capacity expanded to 1,400. (*Sun-Telegraph.*)

The Raiders' first home game on December 6, 1944, should have been seen as an omen. The start was delayed 35 minutes because oil on the court made it too slippery to play, and officials tried to mop the floor, even shooting fire extinguishers on the court to break down the oil. Despite all that, the Raiders beat the Cleveland Allmen 55-53 before a capacity crowd, and things looked promising. (*Post-Gazette*.)

It was downhill from there. The team fell to last in the league and by the end were barely drawing 200 fans for a benefit game to fight polio. After that one miserable season, the franchise suspended operations and never returned. This is a side view of the Duquesne gym with an outdoor recreation area on the roof. (DUA.)

In 1946–1947, the Basketball Association of America (BAA) was formed to compete with the National Basketball League. The Pittsburgh Ironmen, with The Gardens as their home, were a charter franchise in the new league. Here they are at their first home game. (*Post-Gazette.*)

The 1946–1947 season was busy at The Gardens with pro hockey and basketball, public skating, and an Ice Follies. Sadly, the Ironmen continued the miserable history of Pittsburgh's pro basketball teams by finishing last with a 15-45 record and folding. In 1949, the BAA absorbed the NBL and was renamed the National Basketball Association (NBA). The current NBA includes the BAA in its statistics, and the Ironmen's only season ranks among the league's worst. (*Sun-Telegraph.*)

Construction of the Civic Arena jump-started interest in bringing professional basketball back to Pittsburgh. The NBA awarded an expansion franchise to Gardens owner John Harris in 1960, but Harris declined it. The American Basketball League (ABL) was formed in 1960 and included a Pittsburgh franchise, dubbed the Pittsburgh Renaissance or "Rens" for short. This program cover is from that inaugural year. (AC.)

The Rens began training camp on October 2, 1961, at the Pitt Pavilion, former home court of the Pitt Panthers. Located beneath the ramps at Gate 2 of Pitt Stadium, it seated about 4,000 on wood bleachers. It is seen here during a Civic Light Opera rehearsal. The scoreboard is on the far wall at left. The pavilion had a reputation as uncomfortable and cold as a meat locker. The Rens would be its last tenant. (CLP.)

After a month-long training camp, the Rens went on an exhibition tour of the Midwest with the Kansas City Steers. The Rens then defeated the Hawaii Chiefs in a final exhibition game at Butler High School on November 4, 1961. The Rens tried to make a big splash in their opening week at the Civic Arena with concerts and Globetrotter games. (*Press.*)

Here, the Rens try out the new $14,000 court at the Civic Arena for the first time on November 3, 1961. They opened their regular season at the Civic Arena on November 5 with an 87-82 win over the Cleveland Pipers and a crowd of 6,236. (*Press.*)

As seen in this early view when the facility was new, the arena was not ideal for basketball. Seats at either end of the floor seem far from the action. This was not a big issue for Rens fans, because the crowds the team drew were modest. (MRA.)

The Rens compiled a 41-40 record in 1961–1962, and things looked promising for 1962–1963. The team had two future hall of famers: coach Neil Johnston (second row, far right) and league MVP Connie Hawkins (second row, second from right). Sadly, the ABL succumbed to financial losses and folded on December 31, 1962, completing only half the season. The Rens slipped into obscurity. (AC.)

Pittsburgh was not entirely without pro basketball after the demise of the Rens. From 1963 to 1967, the Philadelphia 76ers played occasional regular-season NBA games at the Civic Arena. In 1967, including six games at the arena, the team won the NBA title with Wilt Chamberlain (seen here) as league MVP. The Cleveland Cavaliers played occasional preseason games here, and the Summer Pro Classic brought NBA stars for exhibition games from 1977 to 1984. (AC.)

With the Pitt Pavilion clearly inadequate as a college venue, the University of Pittsburgh began construction of the Fitzgerald Field House in 1951. Opened December 15, 1951, it served as the home of Pitt basketball for 51 years. Here, the steel frame that defined the arched roof of the building takes shape. (HHC.)

The finished product is packed for an event. The field house seated 5,200 when it opened, with later renovations taking that to 6,798. As of this writing, the building survives as home to Pitt volleyball and wrestling teams, as well as athletic training facilities. (HHC.)

The American Basketball Association (ABA) was founded in 1967 with the Pittsburgh Pipers as an inaugural member. The Pipers used the YMHA gym and Fitzgerald Field House for preseason workouts and scrimmages. The Pipers pose in the field house during their preseason before moving to the Civic Arena for the regular season. Hawkins returned, led the ABA in scoring, and was voted MVP six years after winning the same title with the Rens. (CMOA.)

Hawkins's popularity translated to an average attendance of 3,200 per game with a league-high single-game attendance of 12,300. The Pipers breezed through the playoffs until the finals, when they won Game 7 at the Civic Arena on May 4, 1968. Then, against all reason, the championship team was moved to Minneapolis, where another ABA team had already failed to draw. The 1968–1969 season was an injury-plagued disaster in Minnesota, and the team was forced to move again. (*Post-Gazette*.)

In another baffling move, the Pipers returned to Pittsburgh for the 1969–1970 season, but Hawkins jumped to the NBA. With resentment at ownership and without their popular star, attendance cratered. For 1970–1971, the team was rebranded the Condors. In a desperate attempt to stimulate fan interest, management made all 13,000 tickets to the November 17, 1970, game free. They drew a season-high 8,074 but had nearly 5,000 tickets they could not even give away. (RABA.)

In another view of free ticket night, the scoreboard and lighting array are visible. The Condors lost the game 122-116 and any chance for fan support. In 1971–1972, the team rebranded with a new logo and uniforms and brought the NBA Milwaukee Bucks in for an exhibition game on October 10, 1971. When Bucks star Lew Alcindor sat out with an injury, it angered 8,000 fans. The new-look Condors drew fewer than 1,000 per game. (RABA.)

Coach Jack McMahon seems to sum up Pittsburgh's feelings about the Condors. He was fired 10 games into the 1971–1972 season. By the spring of 1972, the Condors moved "home" games to Uniontown, Pennsylvania; Connellsville, Pennsylvania; Birmingham, Alabama; and Tucson, Arizona. After the season, the ABA folded the franchise. When the ABA merged into the NBA in 1976, the Pittsburgh franchise was long gone, and major-league basketball has never returned to Pittsburgh. (RABA.)

Subsequent minor-league efforts have all failed. In 1994, the Piranhas of the Continental Basketball Association (CBA) played one season in Duquesne University's A.J. Palumbo Center (now the Chuck Cooper Center), drawing only 1,600 per game, despite making it to the CBA Championship. The Hard Hats of the second American Basketball Association folded before they even started in 2004. (SAV.)

The Pennsylvania Pit Bulls (ABA) debuted on November 19, 2004, at the Wunderly Gymnasium on the Penn State McKeesport campus. Tragically, coach Tom Washington, a member of the 1967–1968 ABA champion Pipers, suffered a fatal heart attack on the court during that game. Renamed the Xplosion (ABA, CBA), the team folded in 2008. The Pittsburgh Phantoms (ABA) lasted one season, 2009–2010. The Steel City Yellow Jackets (ABA) survived the longest (2014–2023), winning a league championship in 2022. (PSU.)

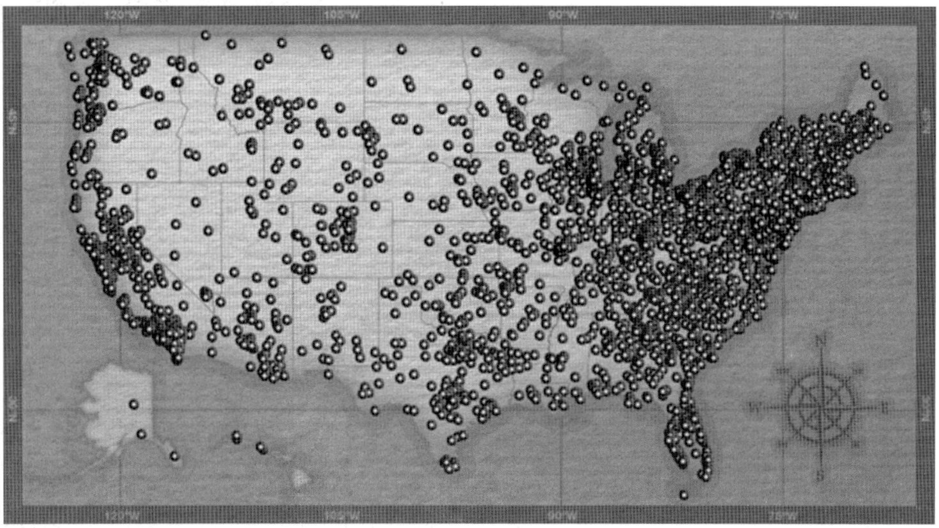

Consistent with our mission to preserve history on a local level, this book was printed in South Carolina on American-made paper and manufactured entirely in the United States. Products carrying the accredited Forest Stewardship Council (FSC) label are printed on 100 percent FSC-certified paper.

MADE IN THE USA